'Little children,
it is the last hour; and as you
have heard that the Antichrist is coming, even
now many antichrists have come, by which we know
that it is the last hour. *They went out from us, but they
were not of us*; for if they had been of us, they would have
continued with us; but they went out that they might be made
manifest, that none of them were of us' (1 John 2:19-19).

Jesus said, "The Kingdom of heaven is like a man who sowed
good seed in his field; but while men slept, his enemy came
and sowed tares among the wheat and went his way. But
when the grain had sprouted and produced a crop, then the
tares also appeared" (Matthew 13:24-26).

'As you therefore have received Christ Jesus the Lord, so walk
in Him, rooted and built up in Him and established in the faith,
as you have been taught, abounding in it with thanksgiving.
Beware lest anyone cheat you through philosophy and
empty deceit, according to the tradition of men,
according to the basic principles of the
world, and not according to Christ'
(Colossian 2:6-8).

Contents

TARES and

WEEDS

In your Church

**Trouble & Deception in God's House
The End Time Overcomers**

**Church Discipline, Christian Leadership
Spiritual Warfare, Presumption
And Defeating the Enemy**

R. B. Watchman

Tares and Weeds in Your Church
Trouble & Deception in God's House, The End Time
Overcomers: Church Discipline, Christian Leadership,
Spiritual Warfare, Presumption and Defeating the Enemy

Copyright © Mathew Backholer 2015, 2017
ByFaith Media - **www.ByFaith.org** - All Rights Reserved -

ISBN 978-1-907066-43-6 (paperback)
ISBN 978-1-907066-44-3 (eBook ePub)

British Library Cataloguing In Publication Data
A Record of this Publication is available from the British Library.
First published in July 2015 by ByFaith Media
and updated in August 2017.

- Jesus Christ is Lord -

Preface

'...Christ in you, the hope of glory. Him we preach, warning every man and teaching every man in all wisdom, that we may present every man perfect in Christ Jesus' (Colossians1:27b-28).

I had been a disciple of Jesus Christ for more than a decade when in a sermon my pastor mentioned 'tares' (also known as weeds in the NIV). After the sermon I asked my pastor to elaborate on the subject of tares. "Every church has a tare," he said, "and you know who the person is in this church." One of the congregation was a troublemaker who always opposed the pastor, sowing discord and was offish, even rude to some members of the congregation. This person attended most church meetings and would often end up being a nuisance. Whilst claiming to be a Christian, he did not live in unity with the other members of the Body of Christ, nor was he prepared to submit to those in leadership and I could not see any fruit of the Spirit in his life.

My pastor's sermon was my first introduction to tares and as the years and decades rolled on, the Holy Spirit began to teach me more about tares, spiritual warfare and being led by the Spirit. At present, I have not heard another sermon on the subject of tares and felt prompted by the Lord to put down what I have learnt into an easy digestible format, so that other disciples of the Lord Jesus Christ can be better informed and therefore better equipped to deal with tares in their lives and ministry.

Much of what I have written is personal, excerpts from my life, combined with scriptural teachings. I also include examples from the various churches I have ministered in, the different church leaders who have sought my counsel, those to whom the Holy Spirit has asked me to intercede for, or to speak into their lives the word of the Lord. Not all troublesome people are tares, the same as not all people need deliverance, but the journey of how people become tares, taken captive to the will of the enemy is revealed and the works of the Devil are exposed. Victory is on the Lord's side, and the how and where of spiritual warfare in the Spirit unfolds, as does my journey of discovery and greater faith in Jesus Christ.

The will of God unfolds through the passages of Scripture and the struggles of the Church in these last days end time battles, when all Christians are called to put on the full armour of God and go out to battle. For our struggle is not against flesh and blood, but against the rulers, against the authorities, against the powers of this dark world, and against spiritual forces of evil in heavenly realms (Ephesians 6:12).

God's intent was that now through the Church, the manifold wisdom of God should be made known to the rulers and authorities in the heavenly realms (Ephesians 3:10-11). Many disciples of the Lord Jesus Christ have understood this command and go to war daily on their knees. Led by the Holy Spirit they fast, pray and intercede, to bind the strong man and pull down his strongholds, releasing angelic forces to do battle with the principalities and powers of darkness (Daniel 10).

The Kingdom of God advances and the Every Creature Commission continues with each generation of disciples, so that the unreached will get an opportunity to hear the good news (Mark 16:15-18, Matthew 28:18-20). Every tribe, nation, tongue and people group will be represented in heaven (Matthew 24:14, 2 Peter 3:12, Revelation 5:9, Revelation 7:9), to the praise and glory of God. Tares are planted to ultimately resist this being fulfilled and to get God's people to disobey or be distracted from the will of God for their lives. This is why the Church needs to know what a tare is, how to recognise them in our churches and lives, and how to neutralise them in the love and peace of the Holy Spirit.

Introduction

Jesus said, "The Kingdom of heaven is like a man who sowed good seed in his field; but while men slept, his enemy came and sowed tares among the wheat and went his way. But when the grain had sprouted and produced a crop, then the tares also appeared. So the servants of the owner came and said to him, 'Sir, did you not sow good seed in your field? How then does it have tares?' He said to them, 'An enemy has done this.' The servants said to him, 'Do you want us then to go and gather them up?' But he said, 'No, lest while you gather up the tares you also uproot the wheat with them. Let both grow together until the harvest, and at the time of harvest I will say to the reapers, "First gather together the tares and bind them in bundles to burn them, but gather the wheat into my barn" ' " (Matthew 13:24-30).

Jesus Christ warned that in His Church there will be seeds of many different kinds (Matthew 13:3-30). There will be those who fall away quickly or whose faith dries up, there will be young Christians needing to mature, undisciplined believers living in the flesh, whilst others will be fruit-bearing and discerning. Then there are the tares also known as weeds, (enemies of God), who pretend to be the wheat (Christians) that have been sown by the enemy (the Devil) and grow up with the wheat.

Jesus did not say everything in His Church would be in perfect harmony, but He is coming back for a pure and spotless Bride (the Church). He warned that tares, which manifest themselves as religious people and posing as Christians, will be sent by the enemy to try and stop God's will being fulfilled in people's lives, and in the Church at large. Why did Jesus warn us that His Church would come under attack from within? So we can be prepared, act, weaken and neutralise the enemy! The subject of tares is not a issue that receives much attention. Many Christians have not heard about them, or believe them to be non-Christians involved in politics, governments or other institutions, or even immigrants from other countries of different religions. Most Christians will not have heard a sermon on the subject of tares and when Jesus spoke a parable on the subject of tares (Matthew 13:24-30), even the Twelve Disciples had to ask for an explanation.

'Jesus sent the multitude away and went into the house. And His disciples came to Him, saying, "Explain to us the parable of the tares of the field." He answered and said to them, "He who sows the good seed is the Son of Man. The field is the world, the good seeds are the sons of the Kingdom, but the tares are the sons of the wicked one. The enemy who sowed them is the Devil, the harvest is the end of the age, and the reapers are the angels. Therefore as the tares are gathered and burned in the fire, so it will be at the end of this age. The Son of Man will send out His angels, and they will gather out of His Kingdom all things that offend, and those who practice lawlessness, and will cast them into the furnace of fire. There will be wailing and gnashing of teeth. Then the righteous will shine forth as the sun in the Kingdom of their Father. He who has ears to hear, let him hear!" ' (Matthew 13:36-43).

Consider the following examples to help explain and reveal what a tare is and how they operate in the setting of a church (or even in a Bible College/Seminary or a Christian ministry!).

Pastor John has been leading his local church for a decade. For the last two years, the Lord has been speaking to Pastor John about allowing the Holy Spirit to take a greater role in the services. The church is in decline and Pastor John has been praying for a way forward. Having received many confirmations from God and knowing that it is biblical, the pastor has changed the way services are organised. He has been teaching his congregation about the fruit and gifts of the Holy Spirit, and has made space in the meetings for the Holy Spirit to move. There is only one problem.

Betty has been a member of this church for six years. She is hard working, she tithes and attends all the meetings. Betty is also the inspirer and ring-leader of a rebellion against this change. She has orchestrated a movement to resist the ministry of the Holy Spirit in the church and has turned many once opened hearts, against the transformation. Despite this, the church is now growing and new-life is flowing, but always behind the scenes, the former bedrock of the church, Betty, is fighting to get 'her church' back to the way it once was.

In another example, Peter has led many people to faith in Jesus Christ and the Lord has been leading him to leave his work to become a full-time evangelist. However, his best friend Anthony is set against it. Anthony attends the same church as Peter and yet he has done everything in his power to undermine Peter's calling. Anthony often reminds Peter of the financial implications of the call and has told him that others are better suited and more qualified for such an undertaking. Peter is not sure what to do. Should he listen to Anthony who tells him he is not qualified, called or ready, or should he heed the Spirit's inner witness within? Is God speaking through Anthony or is it someone else?

Consider another example. Louise was once on-fire and moving forward in her faith in Christ. She was full of enthusiasm and ready to pay the price to walk into God's call. But things have radically changed in the last two years. Louise met Piper at church and after hearing of all of Piper's problems, Louise felt it was her Christian duty to do all she could to help. Louise stopped attending the prayer meetings, so she could pray with Piper and counsel her. Louise started giving her tithe to Piper to help pay her rent, and she felt compelled to assist Piper whenever she needed more. Louise is now exhausted. It seems the more she gives to Piper, the more Piper needs, and Louise just doesn't have the strength and fire to pursue God like she used to. She is now worn-out and worn-down. Everyone in the church has witnessed the change in Louise and the negative effect Piper has had on her. Nevertheless, Louise feels it is her Christian duty to keep on giving and never give up on someone in need, regardless of the failure of Piper to change for the better.

These stories are parables, based upon real-life experiences and they begin to shed light on the work of a tare. A tare does not enter a church wearing a red suit, holding a pitchfork, with a sign stating, "I'm here to undermine and destroy God's work." A tare enters as a friendly face coming to give, to assist in any way he or she can, or a tare can be one in need of endless help, but who is not prepared to do their bit. The "friendly" tare goes on to build a foundation as 'one of God's people,' but begins to undermine what God is doing from within. The tare with an endless need will try to drain the life and energy from those around them, especially the leadership, and will try to undermine all that is positive within a church, Bible College/Seminary, Christian ministry or Christian community etc.

The work of a tare can be most confusing, because the leader, elders, deacons, or church members can be bewildered. On one hand the tare shows signs of religious commitment, on the other hand, he or she is resolutely opposed to the existing or new thing God is doing. They are friend and foe, follower and leader, religious and antichrist. You know there is something wrong with them and yet, you just cannot put your finger on it.

Tares are not outside of God's work, they are on the inside! Jesus said, "The Son of Man will send out His angels and they will gather *out of His Kingdom* all things that offend" (Matthew 13:41). Today there are tares working within churches, Bible Colleges and Christian ministries! However, the good news is that God has given us the ability to discern, weaken and neutralise them, for His glory and for the expansion of His Kingdom. Do not be discouraged, be empowered, because tares are on the losing side!

Chapter One

Tares – Enemies of God

'The solid foundation of God stands, having this seal, "The Lord knows those who are His," and, "Let everyone who names the name of Christ depart from iniquity." But in a great house there are not only vessels of gold and silver, but also of wood and clay, some for honour and some for dishonour' (2 Timothy 2:19).

Jesus spoke of tares (also known as weeds in the NIV) who grow with the wheat, who will be separated at the end of the age (Matthew 13:24-26). Tares are often experts in the act of infiltration, misinformation, deceit and deception. They act the part, sound the part and will blend in very well at any church meeting, Bible College/Seminary or Christian ministry, but it is not until the harvest that they are truly exposed for what they are – tares and not wheat, and they will be burned whilst the wheat will be gathered into God's barn (Matthew 13:24-30). Jude notes false teachers who were so well disguised that they even participated in the 'love feasts,' but only ministered for their own financial gain, being 'clouds without rain, carried about by the winds; late autumn trees, twice dead, pulled up by the roots; raging waves of the sea, foaming up their shame; wandering stars for whom is reserved the blackness of darkness for ever' (Jude 12-13).

Jesus stated that the road to destruction is very broad, but narrow is the gate that leads to eternal life and there are few who find it (Matthew 7:13-14). Some people are taken captive by the Devil to do his will (2 Timothy 2:26), their very conscience has been 'seared with a hot iron' as they give 'heed to deceiving spirits and doctrines of demons' (1 Timothy 4:1-3). Thus rendering them unable to discern between the holy and the unholy, the clean and the unclean (Leviticus 10:10). More often than not they will call 'evil good and good evil; who put darkness for light and light for darkness' and 'put bitter for sweet and sweet for bitter' and woe unto them! (Isaiah 5:20).

Whenever you do the work of God you can expect opposition, even when the work is going well and bearing fruit. The Bible is full of instances where the enemy is aroused at the things of God, and pours out his vengeance through men and women against God's servants. The prophet Micaiah was punched on the cheek for telling the prophets via the Lord that they had a lying spirit and were therefore deceived. Jezebel killed hundreds of the Lord's prophets and followers; Jeremiah was put in the stocks and also placed in a dried up well and his messages from the Lord were ignored for twenty-three years as he spoke the Word of God. Jesus was whipped, beaten and then crucified, and Stephen became the first Christian martyr. The apostle Paul was stoned, whipped, beaten and imprisoned on numerous occasions.

Enemies of God, haters of the cross of Christ are scattered throughout the Bible (Philippians 3:18), and engraved on the pages of Church history, therefore should we expect it to be any different today?

Enemies, Deceivers and Those Who Strayed
- Various kings of Egypt (Exodus 1:12-14, Exodus 5:14).
- Korah, Dathan, Abiram and On, Israelites, rebelled against Moses' leadership and they died by the hand of God alongside their families (Numbers 16:1-35).
- Tobiah and Sanballat tried to lure Nehemiah into a trap and even sent letters to try to frighten him (Nehemiah 2:19, Nehemiah 6:1-19).
- Geshem the Arab despised the Jews, laughed them to scorn and tried to do mischief against Nehemiah (Nehemiah 2:19, Nehemiah 6:2).
- Jannes and Jambres resisted Moses (2 Timothy 3:8).
- Jesus spoke about the Jews' forefathers who shed the blood of the prophets (Matthew 23:29-33).
- King Herod tried to kill the promised King, the Messiah and ordered the death of all the males in Bethlehem who were aged two or under (Matthew 2:16).
- Judas betrayed Jesus (Matthew 26:14-16, 47-49).

- Simon the sorcerer was converted and baptised during a time of revival! He tried to buy the ability to impart the Holy Spirit. Peter declared, "Your heart is not right in the sight of God...you are poisoned by bitterness and bound by iniquity" (Acts 8:9-23).
- Hymenaeus and Alexander 'suffered shipwreck' after rejecting the faith (1 Timothy 1:19-20).
- Hymenaeus (as above) and Philetus strayed concerning the truth, and spread malicious lies thus overthrowing the faith of some (2 Timothy 2:16-18).
- Demas 'having loved this present world' forsook the apostle Paul (2 Timothy 4:10).
- Alexander the coppersmith did the apostle Paul much harm and resisted his words (2 Timothy 4:14-15).
- Some professing believers are insubordinate, they are deceivers who profess to know God 'but by their works deny Him' (Titus 1:10-11, 18).
- Diotrephes, a self-promoting leader of the church told his congregation lies and expelled those who followed elder John (3 John 9-19).[1]

Saul (later renamed Paul), believed he was doing the work of God, persecuting the followers of Christ, dragging them to prison and he consented to the death of Stephen, the first Christian Martyr (Acts 7:54-60, Acts 8:1-3). Saul was on his way to Damascus to arrest Christians when a flash of light blinded him and he fell to the ground. Whilst on the floor, Jesus asked him, "Why are you persecuting Me?" 'Trembling and astonished' Saul asked what he should do and when he opened his eyes he was unable to see (Acts 10:1-9). Saul's conversion transformed his life forever, from persecuting followers of 'the Way,' he began to preach Jesus Christ as the Saviour of the world. Paul persecuted the church, not because he was a tare, but because he was ill-informed and deceived.

The apostle Paul and Barnabas were on their first missionary journey and they encountered opposition in most of the places they went, from both Jews and Gentiles, the religious and the non-religious.

Paul preached in the synagogue in Antioch in Pisidia with great success, 'many of the Jews and devout proselytes' heeded their message (Acts 13:14-43). On the following

Sabbath, 'almost the whole city came together to hear the Word of God' but the Jews seeing the multitudes 'were filled with envy; and contradicting and blaspheming, they opposed the things spoken by Paul.' Both Paul and Barnabas 'grew bold' and stated that as the Jews rejected the truth they would 'turn to the Gentiles' and more people were won to the Lord. 'But the Jews stirred up the devout and prominent women and the chief men of the city, raised up persecution against Paul and Barnabas and expelled them from their region' (Acts 13:44-52). These people were religious unbelieving tares and persecutors.

At Iconium, Paul and Barnabas entered the synagogue and preached the Word of the Lord and 'a great number of multitudes of Jews and Greeks believed. But the unbelieving Jews stirred up the Gentiles and poisoned their minds against the brethren.' They stayed there a long time preaching with signs and wonders following. But 'the multitude of the city was divided; part sided with the Jews, and part with the apostles.' But when both Jews and Gentiles violently attempted 'to abuse and stone them' they fled to the cities of Lycaonia (Acts 14:1-6).

Paul and Silas went into the synagogue in Thessalonica and preached. A great multitude of devout Greeks and many of the leading women followed them, which led to a riot. The people said, "These who have turned the world upside down have come here too" (Acts 17:1-9).

Paul and Silas were sent to Berea and they preached in the synagogue. Many believed, both Greeks and prominent women of the city, but Jews from Thessalonica stirred up the crowd and another riot began! (Acts 17:10-15).

Paul preached on Mars Hill, in the midst of the Areopagus in Athens to the pagans, 'some mocked,' but 'some men joined him and believed' (Acts 17:22-34). Paul also taught in the school at Tyrannus for two years and all who dwelt in Asia (Minor) heard the Word of the Lord, both Jews and Greeks, but 'some were hardened' and 'spoke evil of the Way' (Acts 19:8-9).[2]

The apostles and early Christians received tremendous opposition and persecution in their day, yet were able to keep focused on the task at hand, to proclaim the good news and to walk in the Spirit showing forth the love of Christ.

Chapter Two

The Farmer and his Seed

Jesus said, "So the servants of the owner came and said to him, 'Sir, did you not sow good seed in your field? How then does it have tares?' " (Matthew 13:27).

About a decade ago, it pleased the Holy Spirit to bring me into contact with a Christian agricultural farmer. I enquired if he could give me any help in understanding tares, and how they can grow alongside the good seed. He shared with me that when the price of organic grown oats were at an all-time high, it made good fiscal sense to grow them, knowing he would receive a good return on his investment. He gave considerable thought to this and purchased the finest certified seeds available. This provided the assurance of the seed purity and quality, which would in turn, provide a high yield. He ploughed his fields and gave great attention to the preparation of the soil, then he sowed the seeds.

The farmer was very encouraged as the seeds germinated and grew stronger than he anticipated. As the oats formed heads and matured, he noticed that there were patches of wild oats growing alongside his finest oats. No oats had ever been grown in these fields in living memory, wild or otherwise, but there they were, much to his vexation. The farmer explained to me that only in the last days before the harvest was he able to see the difference. When he tried to remove the wild oats by hand, they shed their seed, making matters worse for future and subsequent years.

All modern day edible cereals: wheat, barley, oats, corn etc. would have come from an original wild source, and it is the same with tares. No matter what denomination your church is affiliated to, if any, with few exceptions, in all probability you will have at least one tare in your midst, but especially if your denomination has already rejected the Holy Spirit and/or rejected the express will of God as revealed in the Bible on the issues of: marriage, between a man and a woman, or one's sexual orientation, or the sin of: adultery, abortion, euthanasia, fornication, drunkenness, lying or greed etc.

Alopecurus myosuroides is an annual grass, a weed and is a major problems to farmers who grow cereal crops. In the UK, this grass is known as black-grass. It can grow at a very high density and will compete against the crops that the farmer has sown, and will reduce the yield of crops, especially barley or wheat. Black-grass sheds a large amount of seed before the crop is cut and has developed resistance to different herbicides, which used to be able to deal with it. Some farmers will burn their entire crop (acres upon acres) with herbicides to eradicate black-grass from their fields, at a large financial loss to themselves. Christians take note: Farmers know the importance of dealing with invasive weeds, to ignore it, is to invite more trouble. The Home Grown Cereals Authority (HGCA) founded in 1965 in the UK, states: 'No two farms are the same, so the approach needs to be tailored to the conditions in the fields on that farm.'[1] It is the same with tares.

When Jesus was teaching His followers about Himself, and it was hard teaching, many of them turned away from Him and followed Him no more (John 6:66). Jesus then asked the Twelve Disciples if they wished to leave. Peter said, "Lord, to whom shall we go? You have the words of eternal life. Also we have come to believe and know that You are the Christ, the Son of the living God." Jesus answered them, "Did I not choose you, the twelve, and one of you is a Devil?" (John 6:67-70). Judas was an apostle/disciple, yet after the Devil had entered him (Luke 22:3), he betrayed Jesus for thirty pieces/coins of silver. Ask yourself, is the Holy Spirit and all His gifts welcome, encouraged and operating in your church or denomination? If not, why not, have you sold Him, like Judas sold Jesus? If the Holy Spirit is not welcome in your church, ministry or your denomination, then who or what has taken His place? You may claim to believe in the Holy Spirit, but do you embrace Him? Do you quench, grieve or resist the Holy Spirit? The Holy Spirit can be 'quenched,' 'grieved' or 'resisted,' all of which are forbidden in Scripture (1 Thessalonians 5:19, Ephesians 4:30, Acts 7:51). Whilst we are commanded to be 'filled with the Spirit,' to 'walk in the Spirit,' be 'led of the Spirit,'

(Ephesians 5:18, Galatians 5:16, 25, Romans 8:14), and He is 'given to those who obey Him' (Acts 5:32).[2] We are told 'submit to God' and 'resist the Devil' (James 4:7), however if we resist the Holy Spirit then we are in league with the Devil, submitting to him and his evil ways!

The apostle Paul wrote to the Church at Ephesus: 'I, therefore, the prisoner of the Lord, beseech you to walk worthy of the calling with which you were called, with all lowliness and gentleness, with longsuffering, bearing with one another in love, endeavouring to keep the unity of the Spirit in the bond of peace. There is one body and one Spirit, just as you were called in one hope of your calling; one Lord, one faith, one baptism; one God and Father of all, who is above all, and through all, and in you all' (Ephesians 4:1-6).

Verses 4-6 mentions the one Spirit, the one Lord and the one God – the Trinity, but do you embrace all three? They are all One in Spirit and in truth and we must all abide with Them. Only eleven of the original apostles/disciples continued to abide with Jesus. After Jesus had washed their feet, He comforted them and promised to send the Holy Spirit. Eleven times, Jesus warned them to continue to abide. He told them this so that they would not go astray (John 13-16).

Jesus said, "Therefore I say to you, every sin and blasphemy will be forgiven men, but the blasphemy against the Spirit will not be forgiven men. Anyone who speaks a word against the Son of Man, it will be forgiven him; but whoever speaks against the Holy Spirit, it will not be forgiven him, either in this age or in the age to come" (Matthew 12:31-32).

Jesus said, "Assuredly, I say to you, all sins will be forgiven the sons of men, and whatever blasphemies they may utter; but he who blasphemes against the Holy Spirit never has forgiveness, but is subject to eternal condemnation" (Mark 3:28-29).

Jesus said, "Well did Isaiah prophesy of you hypocrites, as it is written: 'This people honours Me with their lips, but their heart is far from Me. And in vain they worship Me, teaching as doctrines the commandments of men' " (Mark 7:5-7).

Jesus has warned us about speaking against the Holy Spirit, the unpardonable sin, and putting our traditions before Him. Having shared with His disciples all they needed to know about the Holy Spirit, who would continue Jesus' work on earth through them, He said, "These things I have spoken to you, that you should not be made to stumble" (John 16:1), which the NIV renders: "…so that you will not go astray." Many have rejected the Holy Spirit, His gifts, His ministry and have been led astray, they have stumbled, and this is the work of tares – to make Christians stumble and to lead them astray.

If you, your church fellowship, ministry or denomination are not under the Lordship of Jesus Christ and being led by the Holy Spirit, then there is every possibility that you are led by your traditions, some of which may have been introduced by antichrist spirits working through tares!

"And it shall come to pass in the last days," says God, "that I will pour out of My Spirit on all flesh; your sons and your daughters shall prophesy, your young men shall see visions, your old men shall dream dreams" (Acts 2:17). The Devil working through tares will do all they can to stop you receiving Him. I have been shocked and grieved by so many down the years who claim to be disciples and love the Lord Jesus Christ, yet at the same time, are hostile towards the Holy Spirit of God. Jesus has warned us of taking just any road of our choosing and broad is the road that leads to destruction (Matthew 7:13-23).

Then one said to Jesus, "Lord, are there few who are saved?" And He said to them, "Strive to enter through the narrow gate, for many, I say to you, will seek to enter and will not be able. When once the Master of the house has risen up and shut the door, and you begin to stand outside and knock at the door, saying, 'Lord, Lord, open for us,' and He will answer and say to you, 'I do not know you, where you are from, then you will begin to say, 'We ate and drank in Your presence, and You taught in our streets. But He will say, 'I tell you I do not know you, where you are from. Depart from Me, all you workers of iniquity' " (Luke 13:23-27).

As I look back on my life, I can now see clearly how I was groomed by a tare into a counterfeit friendship over a long period of time. Slowly but surely, I was deceived into believing that my friend had my best interests at heart. Because he was so deceived, he really believed he was acting in God's best interests and mine (like Saul, the persecutor of Christians), but how wrong was he! I share more on this in subsequent chapters.

Chapter Three

Tares and Weeds Explained

Jesus said, "The Kingdom of heaven is like a man who sowed good seed in his field; but while men slept, his enemy came and sowed tares among the wheat and went his way. But when the grain had sprouted and produced a crop, then the tares also appeared" (Matthew 13:24-26).

Jesus was betrayed by Judas (Luke 22:21), one of His apostles/disciples (Matthew 10:2-4), so we should not be surprised when someone close to us does the same. The subject of tares, for some, will be difficult and complex to understand. If God has members of the Body of Christ, who are truly committed to Him, then it follows that the Devil will have counterfeited the same (2 Corinthians 11:14). The Bible calls these people tares and weeds (Matthew 13:36-38). The apostle John warned: 'Little children, it is the last hour; and as you have heard that the Antichrist is coming, even now many antichrists have come, by which we know that it is the last hour. *They went out from us, but they were not of us*; for if they had been of us, they would have continued with us; but they went out that they might be made manifest, that none of them were of us' (1 John 2:18-19).

You may be familiar with the term church plant, or church planting; the apostles planted churches, as do some missionaries. Tares are Devil plants. Satan plants them in churches, fellowships in Christian ministries, denominations, Bible Colleges/Seminaries etc. Jesus explained it in a parable. He said, "The Kingdom of heaven is like a man who sowed good seed in his field; but while men slept, his enemy came and sowed tares among the wheat and went his way. But when the grain had sprouted and produced a crop, then the tares [or weeds] also appeared. So the servants of the owner came and said to him, 'Sir, did you not sow good seed in your field? How then does it have tares?' He said to them, 'An enemy has done this.' The servants said to him, 'Do you want us then to go and gather them up?' But he said, 'No, lest while you gather up the tares you also uproot the wheat with them. Let both grow together until the harvest and at the time of harvest I will say to the reapers, 'First gather together the tares and bind them in bundles to burn them, but gather the wheat into my barn' " (Matthew 13:24-30).

'Then Jesus sent the multitude away and went into the house and His disciples came to Him, saying, "Explain to us the parable of the tares of the field." He answered and said to them, "He who sows the good seed is the Son of Man. The field is the world, the good seeds are the sons of the Kingdom, but the tares are the sons of the wicked one. The enemy who sowed them is the Devil, the harvest is the end of the age, and the reapers are the angels. Therefore, as the tares are gathered and burned in the fire, so it will be at the end of this age. The Son of Man will send out His angels, and they will *gather out of His Kingdom* all things that offend, and those who practice lawlessness and will cast them into the furnace of fire. There will be wailing and gnashing of teeth. Then the righteous will shine forth as the sun in the Kingdom of their Father. He who has ears to hear, let him hear!" ' (Matthew 13:36-43).

As a general rule, tares are so deceived and deluded, that they are not aware of it. This is why tares can think they are part of God's Kingdom, when all their actions prove they serve another (1 John 2:15-17). As they deceive others, so they are deceived themselves: 'Impostors will grow worse and worse, deceiving and being deceived' (2 Timothy 3:13). Tares arise when 'religious-minded' people give their will over to the will of evil spirits (also known as demons, devils etc.); and just as the Holy Spirit seeks a body to live in and work through, so does the Devil, through antichrist spirits. These spirits are literally antagonists of Christ, enemies of the Lord and Christianity; but they live and work through people who, outwardly at least, are not against Jesus Christ or Christianity. These weaker antichrist spirits who find homes in rebellious religious people are part of the preparation for the Antichrist and the false church (2 Thessalonians 2:3). Jesus is coming back to reign for a millennium on earth, and Hitler with the Nazi regime and others wanted to have their own counterfeit millennial reign. Some believe that the Devil himself, entered Hitler as he did Judas two millennia ago.

Jesus warned that in the last days, there will be wars, famines, pestilences, earthquakes and great persecution (Matthew 24:6-10). Then the Lord said, "Many will be offended, will betray one another and will hate one another. Then many false prophets will rise up and deceive many. And because lawlessness will abound, the love of many will grow cold" (Matthew 24:10-14). The Lord clearly states in verse 10, that *many*, not a few, will turn away, *betray* and *hate* others. In verse 12, the Lord tells us *the love of many will grow cold*, many, not the few.

In 2 Thessalonians 1, reference is made concerning Jesus' second coming. It will not happen until the rebellion, falling away or apostasy occurs. This is the deliberate rejection of God's truth; and from it will emerge a true Church and a false church, filled with people like you and me, one will be on the Lord's side, another on the Devil's side; and yet both will be outwardly religious (1 Timothy 1:19-20, 2 Timothy 4:10). Jude explained that these religious people will be spiritually empty and will produce terrible fruit (Jude 12-13).

There are many people who profess to be Christians or disciples of Jesus Christ, yet they are not. They are regular church-goers and may be knowledgeable in the Scriptures, moving in the gift of the Spirits, whilst some may cast out demons and move in signs and wonders, yet they are not part of God's Kingdom! Consider the following Scriptures:

- Jesus said, "By their fruits you will know them. Not everyone who says to Me, 'Lord, Lord,' shall enter the Kingdom of heaven, but he who does the will of My Father in heaven. Many will say to Me in that day, 'Lord, Lord, have we not prophesied in Your name, cast out demons in Your name, and done many wonders in Your name?' And then I will declare to them, 'I never knew you; depart from Me, you who practice lawlessness!' " (Matthew 7:20-23).

- Jesus said, "The Kingdom of heaven is like a man who sowed good seed in his field; but while men slept, his enemy came and sowed tares among the wheat and went his way. ...Let both grow together until the harvest, and at the time of harvest I will say to the reapers, 'First gather together the tares and bind them in bundles to burn them, but gather the wheat into my barn.' "Therefore as the tares are gathered and burned in the fire, so it will be at the end of this age. The Son of Man will send out His angels, and *they will gather out of His Kingdom all things that offend, and those who practice lawlessness*, and will cast them into the furnace of fire. There will be wailing and gnashing of teeth" (Matthew 13:24-25, 30, 40-42).

- Jesus said, "Again, the Kingdom of heaven is like a dragnet that was cast into the sea and *gathered some of every kind,* which, when it was full, they drew to shore; and they sat down and gathered the good into vessels, but threw the bad away. So it will be at the end of the age. The angels will come forth, separate the wicked from among the just, and cast them into the furnace of fire. There will be wailing and gnashing of teeth" (Matthew 13:47-50).

- In the parable of the wedding feast, Jesus said, "Go into the highways, and as many as you find, invite to the wedding. So those servants went out into the highways and gathered together all whom they found, both bad and good. And the wedding hall was filled with guests. But when the king came in to see the guests, *he saw a man there who did not have on a wedding garment*. So he said to him, 'Friend, *how did you come in here without a wedding garment?*' And he was speechless. Then the king said to the servants, 'Bind him hand and foot, take him away, and cast him into outer darkness; there will be weeping and gnashing of teeth.' For many are called, but few are chosen" (Matthew 22:9-14).

- 'Since it is a righteous thing with God...to give you who are troubled rest with us when the Lord Jesus is revealed from heaven with His mighty angels, in flaming fire taking vengeance on those who do not know God, *and on those who do not obey the gospel of our Lord Jesus Christ* [people who profess to be Christians]. These shall be punished with everlasting destruction from the presence of the Lord and from the glory of His power, when He comes, in that Day, to be glorified in His saints and to be admired among all those who believe...' (2 Thessalonians 1:6-10).

Proverbs 7 is about keeping one's self away from the immoral woman, which is equally true about an immoral man. The first four verses are about protecting one's self: treasuring God's Word within you, keeping God's commandments and having wisdom and understanding. Without these traits you are setting yourself up to fail or fall. The way that the adulterous woman is described (verses 5-27), is strikingly similar in the way in which tares also operate.

- She flatters with her words (v5).
- She preys among the weak or those devoid of understanding (v7).
- She has a crafty heart (v10).
- She lurks, seeking who is the best person to catch (verses 12-13).
- She has an appearance of being religious, she has her peace offerings with her (part of Jewish observance, see Leviticus 7:11-21), and has come to pay her vows (v14).
- She came and sought out the person she wanted to commit sin with, she diligently came and met the person (v15).
- She has done her preparation, everything is ready for the illicit union (verses 16-17).
- She has enticing speech and with flattering lips seduced the person into doing what she wanted (v21).
- The person was caught in her web of destruction, and went after her as a ox to the slaughter, or as a fool to the correction of stocks (v22).
- To be forewarned is to be forearmed and the end of Proverbs 7 reveals: 'Now therefore, listen to me, my children; pay attention to the words of my mouth. Do not let your heart turn aside to her ways, do not stray into her paths; for she has cast down many wounded, and all who were slain by her were strong men. Her house is the way to hell, descending to the chambers of death' (verses 24-27).

The book of Proverbs is all about wisdom, read it regularly and apply its teachings. Christians in general and the Church at large, should be full of godly wisdom, however, many lack wisdom. Why invite a stranger to help at the Sunday School or be an usher on the door when they have only come once or twice before? Why invite a person to be on the eldership team when he has only been in the fellowship for a few months? These are not unknown occurrences, but are sadly all too familiar in many congregations. How many people have been given positions of influence or authority and yet you do not know their Christian testimony? How many people say they are a Christian, yet they have never spoken of their conversion experience? Many of whom are still unregenerate, yet they think they are saved! They have not repented of their sins, nor forsaken them, they have not put their trust and faith in the finished work of Jesus Christ. They are not born-again, they are not sealed with the Holy Spirit, they have no assurance from the Spirit of God, they are not children of God and have not passed from death to life. Do you want these type of people assisting or working in your church fellowship? It would be very unwise and will lead to problems. It is not a crime to ask someone about their Christian testimony and experiences.

Only the Holy Spirit knows those who are Christ's wheat or the Devil's tares, but if the Holy Spirit is not welcomed in any building or meeting of believers, how can they claim that it is God's house? If the body of a man is dead without its spirit, then it follows that a church without the Holy Spirit is also dead. In addition, if you reject the Holy Spirit, then you are more vulnerable to receive other spirits!

If you lack wisdom, then ask God for more and ask in faith without doubting (James 1:5-8). There is also the gift of wisdom, 'the word of wisdom' given by the Holy Spirit, which should be exercised when needs arise, alongside the 'discerning of spirits' (1 Corinthians 12:8, 10).

Rev. Duncan Campbell said, "We don't need churches filled with people, but people filled with God!" If you have not got the Holy Spirit, then who or what do you have? Are you a disciple of Jesus Christ who moves in the gifts of the Holy Spirit or are you a church-goer with the nickname Christian? Remember, without the Holy Spirit you (and your fellowship) are at the mercy of the Devil and he has no mercy!

Chapter Four

Enemy Infiltration

Nehemiah came to Jerusalem 'and discovered the evil that Eliashib had done for Tobiah, in preparing a room for him in the courts of the house of God. And it grieved me bitterly; therefore I threw all the household goods of Tobiah out of the room. Then I commanded them to cleanse the rooms.... So I contended with the rulers, and said, "Why is the house of God forsaken?" And I gathered them together and set them in their place' (Nehemiah 13:7-9, 11).

Over the years, I received three great shocks when the Holy Spirit spoke to me about a close friend. We had been friends for decades and I had been meditating on second Thessalonians, concerning the man of lawlessness mentioned in 2 Thessalonians 2, which is another reference to the Antichrist, who will oppose God and set himself up in God's temple. Verse 7 of the same chapter tells us that the secret power of lawlessness is already at work in the world.

We know terrible times will be coming to the true Church and to prepare for this battle, we have been told to watch out for those who cause divisions amongst us, because they are not serving the will of the Lord Jesus Christ, but their own sensual appetites. 'Now I urge you, brethren, note those who cause divisions and offences, contrary to the doctrine which you learned, and avoid them. For those who are such do not serve our Lord Jesus Christ, but their own belly, and by smooth words and flattering speech deceive the hearts of the simple' (Romans 16:17-18). This is what lawlessness is, serving one's own will instead of the will of God, it is rebellion.

I was shocked when the Holy Spirit warned me that my close friend felt contemptuous of me. I defended him, "Never." When I told my friend the exact thing the Holy Spirit had said, he denied it all and by his smooth talk and flattery, what was in him deceived me. I accepted the lie and believed what I wanted to believe, what I was comfortable with. I did not wish to face the truth. I had rejected the truth and it cost me dearly for many years to come. The Holy Spirit cannot and will not lie. The Holy Spirit was so gracious towards me.

In a Contemplation of David (a psalm), he wrote: 'The words of his mouth were smoother than butter, but war was in his heart; his words were softer than oil, yet they were drawn swords' (Psalm 55:21). David wrote of those 'who speak peace to their neighbours, but evil is in their hearts' (Psalm 28:3).

The second shock was unveiled as the Holy Spirit showed me that my close friend was wedded to the world, and was being used by Satan to undermine my call and ministry. We are called to be wedded to Jesus Christ and the will of God, as His Bride, the living Church. He is the Groom. But when I learnt that he was wedded to the world, I thought, 'Oh, this explains so much.'

The apostle John wrote: 'Do not love the world or the things in the world. If anyone loves the world, the love of the Father is not in him' (1 John 2:15). The apostle Paul wrote: '...You also have become dead to the law through the Body of Christ, that you may be *married to another* — to Him who was raised from the dead, that we should bear fruit to God' (Romans 7:4). 'For I am jealous for you with godly jealousy. For *I have betrothed you to one husband,* that I may *present you as a chaste virgin to Christ*' (2 Corinthians 11:2). 'He died for all, that those who live should live no longer for themselves, but for Him who died for them and rose again' (2 Corinthians 5:15). 'You were bought at a price; do not become slaves of men' (1 Corinthians 7:23).

The third and greatest shock stunned me for a moment, when the Spirit told me that my close friend "is a tare, a tool in the hands of the Devil." The Lord showed me that if I was willing, He would teach me more in order that I might share it with others. As part of my teaching, I was led to visit the graves of Rev. Duncan Campbell, Evan Roberts, Sir Winston Churchill, David Lloyd George, T.E. Lawrence, Viscount Montgomery, Rees Howells and Florence Nightingale. All these people knew who their enemies were. Some were spiritual or political, others military or ideological and others were infections and diseases. But the secret was, and still is, knowing who your enemy is. The Bible is very clear about such matters. See Nehemiah 2:10, 19 and Nehemiah 13:4-9.

Many times in the Scriptures God warns of tares and the enemy within, especially as the great spiritual battles ensue, like the end time battles. "Do not trust in a friend; do not put your confidence in a companion; guard the doors of your mouth from her who lies in your bosom. For son dishonours father, daughter rises against her mother, daughter-in-law against her mother-in-law; a man's enemies are the men of his own household" (Micah 7:5-6). Jeremiah the prophet heard the Lord God say, "Everyone take heed to his neighbour and do not trust any brother. For every brother will utterly supplant and every neighbour will walk with slanderers. Everyone will deceive his neighbour and will not speak the truth. They have taught their tongue to speak lies; they weary themselves to commit iniquity. Your dwelling place is in the midst of deceit. Through deceit they refuse to know Me" (Jeremiah 9:4-6).

The Lord Jesus Christ did not come to bring harmony with worldliness, compromise and sin, but to lead us to war in His Kingdom, to destroy the works of the enemy and to set people free from the power of Satan. The Lord said, "Do not think that I came to bring peace on earth. I did not come to bring peace but a sword. For I have come to 'set a man against his father, a daughter against her mother and a daughter-in-law against her mother-in-law,' and 'a man's enemies will be those of his own household.' He who loves father or mother more than Me is not worthy of Me. And he who loves son or daughter more than Me is not worthy of Me" (Matthew 10:34-37).

In all warfare, people have to choose what side they will be on. Jesus said, "Do you suppose that I came to give peace on earth? I tell you, not at all, but rather division. For from now on five in one house will be divided: three against two, and two against three. Father will be divided against son and son against father, mother against daughter and daughter against mother, mother-in-law against her daughter-in-law and daughter-in-law against her mother-in-law" (Luke 12:51-53).

Disciples of Jesus Christ are called to offer their bodies as living sacrifices (Romans 12:1), be led of the Spirit/walk in the Spirit (Romans 8:14, Galatians 5:18, 24-25), and should act in the power of the Spirit (John 14:12, Acts 1:8). Likewise, tares are led to do the same for their master, the Devil, as they have been taken captive to do his will.

Slowly but surely, it was as if spiritual scales were dropping off my eyes, as I received revelation by the Holy Spirit. Tares are sons and daughters of the evil one, sown by the Devil (Matthew 13:38-39). They are assigned to oppose God's servants and to do all they can, to discourage, dishearten, depress or even destroy! Judas was a disciple and the Lord spent a whole night in prayer before he was chosen (Luke 6:12-16), but Judas still betrayed him for thirty silver coins/pieces of silver, and even Satan himself entered him (John 13:27). This man loved money more than Jesus. Judas had been taught by Jesus that, "No one can serve two masters; for either he will hate the one and love the other, or else he will be loyal to the one and despise the other. You cannot serve God and mammon" (Matthew 6:24). Judas was wedded to the world and would fellowship with the Devil, instead of with the Lord.

The Devil is a legalist who has 'legal rights,' but only if we relinquish them by our sin, or the sin of others, especially those in leadership.

The Holy Spirit was so grieved in me on occasions, in some churches or Christian fellowships, by what He and I observed, that I was compelled to speak to the pastor or leaders. I have lost count of the number of times when they replied by saying, "If you are looking for a perfect church, don't go in, you will spoil it." There is some truth in this saying, but it is also a mockery to maintain a status quo which is unacceptable to the Lord, who is holy and commands His Church to be so (1 Peter 1:15-16). See also Matthew 5:48, where Jesus expects His followers to be morally perfect.

Jesus has made it very plain, as the Groom, what He wants His Church, His Bride to be like. 'Husbands, love your wives, just as Christ also loved the Church and gave Himself for her, that He might sanctify and cleanse her with the washing of water by the word, that He might present her to Himself a glorious Church, not having spot or wrinkle or any such thing, but that she should be holy and without blemish' (Ephesians 5:25-27).

The individuals of the Body of Christ are all grafted into God's vine and in John 15, Jesus tells us that God the Father is the Gardener, who prunes out the dead wood in the vine, and puts it on the fire. During the Welsh Revival (1904-1905)[2] so many people came to put their faith in Jesus' death and resurrection that they had to build or enlarge chapels, mission halls and church buildings to gather the harvest. In time, some of the people returned to their own godless ways and many of the religious people returned to their own pious rituals and traditions. As they did, the Holy Spirit departed, the numbers fell and today all over Wales, and the United Kingdom, you will find empty buildings that were once houses of worship, former chapels, churches and mission halls. Now they are homes, offices, mosques, nightclubs, restaurants and shops etc. See Revelation 1:20 and Revelation 2:5.

Already the Devil has his eyes on those who can be groomed from religious Christians into his tares (Isaiah 29:13, Isaiah 46:12), to challenge what God is going to do in the greatest harvest the world has ever seen. Satan had his tares ready in Israel to oppose the coming of the Messiah, the Lord Jesus Christ (Mark 7:6-13). The Pharisees and Sadducees were religious men who claimed they were waiting for the Messiah, but they were the one's who opposed and rejected Him, and sought to kill Him! Jesus said to the Pharisees, "You seek to kill Me, because My word has no place in you. I speak what I have seen with My Father and you do what you have seen with your father." They answered and said to Him, "Abraham is our father." Jesus said to them, "If you were Abraham's children, you would do the works of Abraham. But now you seek to kill Me, a Man who has told you the truth which I heard from God. Abraham did not do this. You do the deeds of your father…. You are of your father the Devil and the desires of your father you want to do. He was a murderer from the beginning and does not stand in the truth, because there is no truth in him. When he speaks a lie, he speaks from his own resources, for he is a liar and the father of it." …Then the Jews answered and said to Him, "Do we not say rightly that You are a Samaritan [a grave cultural insult] and have a demon?" (John 8:37-48).

In the case of Jesus, those who served the Devil made the same accusation against Him! If the true Church is going to counterattack this threat, it is imperative that the Holy Spirit be released in and through those members of the Body of Christ

He has called to be His channels, through whom He can work. The man or woman at the front reaping the harvest cannot fight these battles on his or her own.

In more recent times, some churches have come some way towards what the Lord requires, with leadership teams. In 1 Corinthians 12:13-30, Paul gives teaching to this end. There has to be a spirit of unity, both in the Word and in the Holy Spirit, as verses 13-14 express. The Body of Christ (each individual member), not just the man at the front, must know the Word of truth, the Bible, and the Spirit of Truth. John explained: 'Now by this we know that we know Him, if we keep His commandments' (1 John 2:3). You cannot obey His commands if you do not know them and this is the trouble with the Church, which is made up of many members including you and me – those who have repented and forsaken their former lives of sin, confessed Jesus Christ as their Saviour and Lord, and live for Him. The Lord declared through the prophet Hosea, "My people are destroyed for lack of knowledge" (Hosea 4:6), and, "Let us pursue the knowledge of the Lord" (Hosea 6:3). You must know the Word of God which has been given to us in the Bible, and you must also know the Holy Spirit and His will. The Sword of the Spirit is the Word of God (Ephesians 6:17). This Word, under the direction of the Holy Spirit is living and powerful (Hebrews 4:12), and it can change your life and of those around you!

Tares are well trained in the art of lies, deceit and deception. Most will cloak or cover their words with enough truth to make what they say (or do) palatable. If you meditate on God's Word the Holy Spirit will reveal Jesus' good, pleasing and perfect will to you. Jesus Christ said that all who respond to the gospel must be taught, "To observe all things that I have commanded you" (Matthew 28:20). If you are willing to observe all He teaches, you will grow in the grace of God and get to know the Holy Spirit; if you do not, you may be cut out of the vine and cast into the fire! Jesus said, "If anyone does not abide in Me, he is cast out as a branch and is withered; and they gather them and throw them into the fire, and they are burned" (John 15:6).

The Holy Spirit made it very plain to me that when I turned my back on Him as a young teenager, the enemy assigned a tare to me, which was my future close friend.[1] He was sent into my life to hinder God's work in it. Tares love the world. John commands: 'Do not love the world or the things in the world. If anyone loves the world, the love of the Father is not in him. For all that is in the world – the lust of the flesh, the lust of the eyes, and the pride of life – is not of the Father but is of the world. And the world is passing away, and the lust of it; but he who does the will of God abides forever' (1 John 2:15-17). Because tares love the world, the spirit of the antichrist abides in them (1 John 2:18, 2 John 7). Like the people of Judah in the Old Testament, these tares do not give all their hearts to God, but only in pretence and this opens them up to devils/evil spirits (Jeremiah 3:10). These tares are religious and just go through the outward motions, they are double-minded and unstable in all they do (James 1:7-8).

A tare can be so deceived and deluded that they really believe that God is with them, yet they are fighting against Him, by opposing His servants. 'But evil men and impostors will grow worse and worse, deceiving and being deceived' (2 Timothy 3:13). They can also be wolves in sheep's clothing (Matthew 7:15).

Tares will blend in at any church meeting or even at a Bible College/Seminary, mission or Christian ministry, but it is not until the harvest that they are truly exposed for what they are. Tares will be burned in the fire whilst the wheat will be gathered into God's barn (Matthew 13:24-30). Jude wrote about false teachers who were so well disguised that they even participated in the 'love feasts,' but only ministered for their own financial gain. Being 'clouds without rain, carried about by the winds; late autumn trees, twice dead, pulled up by the roots; raging waves of the sea, foaming up their shame; wandering stars for whom is reserved the blackness of darkness for ever' (Jude 12-13).

The apostle John in his second epistle wrote a warning against false teachers and their messages. John noted that because of the many deceivers and antichrists who claim to be Christian, love must be discerning (2 John 1). This warning of love and discernment notes that you do not blindly and naively offer hospitality to anyone who professes to be a believer – what message do they bring? (verses 9-10). Do they deny Christ as coming in the flesh (v7). Jesus said, "A bad tree cannot bear good fruit" (Luke 6:43-45).

Chapter Five

Captive to Satan

'Avoid foolish and ignorant disputes, knowing that they generate strife. And a servant of the Lord must not quarrel but be gentle to all, able to teach, patient, in humility correcting those who are in opposition, if God perhaps will grant them repentance, so that they may know the truth, and *that they may come to their senses and escape the snare of the Devil, having been taken captive by him to do his will'* (2 Timothy 2:23-26).

In churches and chapels across the world there are: leaders and mature Christians, believers who want to become disciples, rough diamonds being prepared for cleansing and polishing, un-discipled believers, half-hearted nominal Christians, Devil-sent troublemakers, false: teachers, preachers and prophets, and tares. Only God know those who are *truly* His (2 Timothy 2:19), because often we don't! However, the Holy Spirit through the gift of discernment (or a word of knowledge) can reveal to you who is a Saul, waiting to become a Paul, a Demas who will forsake you, or a Judas sent to destroy God's work.

The difference between a tare and a un-discipled believer who *desires* to be more Christ-like can often be discovered through their willingness to embrace repentance, confession and forsaking of sin, and deliverance. Someone who wants to be a true disciple of Jesus Christ will truly repent and will pay the full price to expel the demons that are in or over them. However, a tare will always be half-hearted about confession of sin and repentance. They will never be serious about being free from demonic powers, because they have been taken captive by him to do his will, yet most, if not all, are unaware of this, as they truly believe they are doing the will of God!

The Devil who is the tempter, will search out those who are not fully committed to Jesus Christ in churches and Christian homes, to draw them away from God and back to the world, as the Lord explained in His parable (Matthew 13:19-23). Jesus said, "For where your treasure is, there your heart will be also" (Matthew 6:21).

Demonic forces will do all they can to get church-goers to fellowship with demons, through sin, knowing that the Holy Spirit will depart from them (1 Timothy 4:1). King David, a man after God's own heart knew the danger of this and prayed, "Do not cast me away from Your presence and do not take Your Holy Spirit from me" (Psalm 51:11).

Samson was so deceived that he was unaware that the Lord had left him (Judges 16:20). The Holy Spirit departed from King Saul, as an evil spirit from the Lord tormented him, and even those around him could see and understand what was going on (1 Samuel 16:14-23). It's the same today; demons have infiltrated the Church and taken people captive, just as the apostles said they would (1 Timothy 4:1, 2 Timothy 2:26). These devils are doing all they can to destroy it or at least make it powerless, from within. Lot was tormented in his righteous soul by the lawless deeds he saw and heard in Sodom and Gomorrah (2 Peter 2:7-8), and so are many God-fearing Christians in their churches!

Demons, devils, evil spirits and unclean spirits are synonymous, they are generally one and the same, and are referred to as such in different Bible translations. In relation to demons/evil spirits, Christians and godly people can have, be oppressed, or be under the influence of them (Job 26:4, Mark 1:23-24, 39, Acts 5:3, 2 Timothy 2:24-26, James 3:14-16).

- A 'distressing spirit *from the Lord* came upon [King] Saul' because of his persistent rebellion against the Lord (1 Samuel 19:9). See also 1 Samuel 16:14-15.
- The 'Devil put it into the heart of Judas Iscariot' to betray Jesus, one of the Twelve Disciples! (John 13:2).
- A 'daughter of Abraham' crippled for eighteen years, bent over, kept bound by a spirit of infirmity (Luke 13:10-17). Abraham's children are known as believers (Luke 19:9-10, Galatians 3:7-9), and the implied reference by Jesus was that she believed.

- Peter said that Satan filled Ananias' heart so that he and his wife lied to the Holy Spirit. They were numbered among the believers (Acts 4:32-35). They sold a plot of land and *claimed* to have given all the money to the church (to the Lord via the apostles, to help the poor and needy etc.), but kept some money back and *lied* about it. Both were judged by God and died instantly within hours of each other (Acts 5:1-11).
- Satan desired to sift Peter as wheat (Luke 22:31-32), and he did deny the Lord three times! And repented.
- Demonic forces can attack Christians – hence why Paul said we should have on the full armour of God and take the 'shield of faith' by which we 'will be able to quench all the fiery darts of the wicked one' (Ephesians 6:1-17).
- The apostle Paul received visions, revelations and had been taken up to the third heaven (2 Corinthians 12:1-2). To keep him humble he was given 'a thorn in the flesh, a messenger of Satan to buffet me, lest I be exalted above measure' (2 Corinthians 12:7-10).
- Satan stopped Paul and others from visiting the church at Thessalonica. Paul wrote: 'We wanted to come to you, even I, Paul, time and again – but Satan hindered us' (1 Thessalonians 2:18).

Demonic bondage can range from mild to severe and can cause hardness against the Good News (2 Corinthians 4:4), sinful behaviour (2 Peter 2:1-12), as well as apostasy and false doctrine (1 Timothy 4:1, 1 John 4:1-3).[1]

One part of Satan's strategy to keep people bound is to make the Church and Christians afraid of demons and deliverance. When people say, "I don't want to get involved with that," are they following Jesus' command to cast out demons or following what Satan wants them to think and do, by their inaction and sin of omission? (Mark 16:17). I think it is a part of Satan's strategy to keep people bound, by keeping Christians in fear of demons and making them avoid casting them out. The image we are given in the Bible is not of an all-powerful enemy, but of a defeated foe, with demons trembling at the thought of God (James 2:19, Colossians 1:13, 1 John 3:8). Demonic ruling spirits (strong man) only exist where mankind's sin empowers them, and Christ has given us power to bind these strong men in His name (Matthew 12:29-30). Casting out demons was a central feature of Jesus' ministry and it was absolutely normal for the disciples of Jesus and the apostles to set people free in Jesus' name (Mark 3:15, Mark 6:13, Mark 16:17, Acts 19:12). At least sixty-two times in the Gospels, demons/evil spirits are mentioned, and all true Christians can and must exercise authority over demons in the name of Jesus Christ and command them to go. We can live oppressed by them or master them. It's the same with sin; if you are not the master of it, then you are a slave to it (Romans 6:16). Jesus said, "Most assuredly, I say to you, whoever commits sin is a slave of sin" (John 8:34).

On an individual level, when we plead the blood of Jesus Christ over our lives and we are not living in wilful unrepentant sin (1 John 1:5-10), then the Devil, and his demons have to let us go as they have no legal right or hold over us (1 John 5:18-19). The Advocate, the Lord Jesus Christ, pleads our case and is Himself the propitiation for our sins (1 John 2:1-3). Zechariah 3:1-5 is a strong case example when Joshua the High Priest is standing before the Angel of the Lord and Satan is there accusing him. The Lord rebukes Satan and Joshua's dirty clothes, which represent sin, are replaced with rich robes, which is symbolic of the robes of righteousness, worn by disciples of Jesus Christ because of blood-bought redemption. Christ shed His blood for the forgiveness of our sins and we can claim cleansing by faith in His atoning work on the cross.[2]

Chapter Six

The Form and Nature of Tares

'Now the Spirit expressly says that in latter times some will depart from the faith, giving heed to deceiving spirits and doctrines of demons' (1 Timothy 4:1).

From your very first meeting with some tares, they can radiate the nature of a kindred spirit. This is because they have a powerful spirit of delusion/deception in them and over them. Naturally, it is counterfeit and the opposite of meeting someone who walks with the Holy Spirit in them and over them. There are times when some people have to be handed over to Satan (1 Corinthians 5:5, 1 Timothy 1:19-20), but is only done under the direct instruction of the Holy Spirit.

All evil spirits/demons are at their heart, antichrist and antichristian (Revelation 16:14). The man of lawlessness, which Paul has written of (2 Thessalonians 2:1-12), is yet to be revealed; but he will be a person who has given himself over to Satan. As already mentioned, a tare will have an antichrist spirit abiding in them and working through them.

Paul warned the young pastor Timothy: 'Now the Spirit expressly says that in latter times some will depart from the faith, giving heed to deceiving spirits and doctrines of demons' (1 Timothy 4:1). He also warned him of religious people, having a form of godliness, but they deny its power. 'But know this, that in the last days perilous times will come. For men will be lovers of themselves, lovers of money, boasters, proud, blasphemers, disobedient to parents, unthankful, unholy, unloving, unforgiving, slanderers, without self-control, brutal, despisers of good, traitors, headstrong, haughty, lovers of pleasure rather than lovers of God, having a form of godliness but denying its power. *And from such people turn away!'* (2 Timothy 3:1-5). Have we turned away from them?

Paul warned Timothy that some preachers will turn from the truth and teach fables instead of biblical truth. 'For the time will come when they will not endure sound doctrine, but according to their own desires, because they have itching ears, they will heap up for themselves teachers; and they will turn their ears away from the truth, and be turned aside to fables' (2 Timothy 4:3-4).

John the apostle told the Christians that false spirits will be operating in churches, with false prophets, who are really people committed to the world! We are told we must test the spirits by discerning the message that is shared. Many of these false prophets or teachers etc., will exhort worldly concerns and reject the teaching of the apostles. 'Beloved, do not believe every spirit, but test the spirits, whether they are of God; because many false prophets have gone out into the world. By this you know the Spirit of God. Every spirit that confesses that Jesus Christ has come in the flesh is of God, and every spirit that does not confess that Jesus Christ has come in the flesh is not of God. And this is the spirit of the Antichrist, which you have heard was coming, and is now already in the world. You are of God, little children and have overcome them, because He who is in you is greater than he who is in the world. They are of the world. Therefore, they speak as of the world and the world hears them. We are of God. He who knows God hears us; he who is not of God does not hear us. By this we know the Spirit of Truth and the spirit of error' (1 John 4:1-6). The apostle Paul warned that some people whilst claiming to be Christian have a lower regard for the Bible than other books, or *their* culture, or *their* philosophy that they prefer to exhort, as they preach 'another gospel' and a 'different Jesus' (2 Corinthians 11:3-4, Galatians 1:6-9).

The Devil has a chain of command, similar to a pyramid style of top down leadership. Satan remains at the top and below him are principalities and powers, ruling spirits, evil spirits/demons. This structure was taught by Paul and at their heart, all of them are little antichrists and messengers of Satan (Ephesians 6:12-13).

God has those whom He has set apart from birth and the Devil makes it his business to find out who these people are, so he can oppose and harass them. A tare, that is a person who may be religious but has given themselves over to these evil spirits, even unaware, will have fellowship with demons. They will talk to them. Their bodies will become a counterfeit temple, which the demons work in and through.

These demons can only live in that body by agreement. They abide in them because in the spiritual world they have a legal right (Revelation 12:10). The Devil and his demonic hordes are legalists, they know what their rights are, according to the principles set forth at the beginning of time and they will insist on claiming all that is theirs and adhering to them.

In the book of Job, this righteous man is put to the test when Satan tries every legal trick in the book to get him to sin (Job 1:9-2:10). The high priest Joshua was also subject to a demonic legal attack and the court of heaven ruled in Joshua's favour (Zechariah 3:1-5); a similar situation happened to King David (1 Chronicles 21:1). All these men overcame Satan, but tares give in to him (even unknowingly) and align themselves and their will to his!

The demons in the bodies of tares will have every right to be there, because they were welcomed in, usually unbeknown, but they are there by agreement. They cohabit together. The human and the demon spirits in them live together (Luke 22:3), like a husband and wife, but this is a counterfeit union. You cannot cast them out because the tare is in agreement with them. At the end of the age, Jesus taught He would gather "out of His Kingdom" all those who are lawless and offend Kingdom standards (Matthew 13:24-30, 36-42).

The Lord said, "Therefore as the tares are gathered and burned in the fire, so it will be at the end of this age. The Son of Man will send out His angels and they will gather *out of His Kingdom* all things that offend, and those who practice lawlessness, and will cast them into the furnace of fire. There will be wailing and gnashing of teeth. Then the righteous will shine forth as the sun in the Kingdom of their Father. He who has ears to hear, let him hear!" (Matthew 13:40-43).

When the Holy Spirit abides in you, Jesus said, "He will eat with you and you with Him" (Revelation 3:20). It is the same with tares and demons; only they do the same as a counterfeit. They become good friends, or so the tare is deceived into believing, to undermine God's work.

It is highly unlikely that a tare in a church, fellowship, Bible College or ministry etc., will agree to receive deliverance, but should they, as the host of these demons, you can be sure that the strong man (the ruling spirit who controls them all) will send out one or two lesser, minor demons, to deceive you into thinking the job is done. After sending them out, this ruling spirit will welcome them back later, as the person returns to fellowship with these spirits. As Jesus said, "The last state of that man is worse than the first" (Luke 11:26).

As part of this great deception, a person who is a tare may assist others in casting out demons in other people, as long as the focus does not turn to them (Acts 19:14-17). Jesus taught that people would claim to be His disciples who were not. They would do wonders and cast out demons, yet they do not know Jesus Christ as they "practice lawlessness" (Matthew 7:22-23). The tare will also have a religious spirit, which enables them to hang around the Lord's people, to feed off their spirits and to learn all they can about those who are truly serving the Lord. They do this so that they can direct soulish prayers towards them, which are gratifying to the flesh and demonic in nature (James 3:14-16).

These people may have a spirit of lawlessness operating in them, which means they will always be a law unto themselves. They may have a spirit of rebellion, which is the sin of witchcraft (1 Samuel 15:23). They may have a spirit of selfishness (me, myself and I), and they will have an independent spirit; which will never be truly subject to another because they prefer to be self-reliant.

In the Bible, God reveals the names of many demonic beings:

- A spirit of jealousy (Numbers 5:14).
- Familiar spirit (1 Samuel 28:7).
- Lying spirit (1 Kings 22:22).
- Spirit of haughtiness (Proverbs 16:18-19).
- Perverse spirit (Isaiah 19:14).
- Spirit of slumber (Isaiah 29:10, Romans 11:8).
- Spirit of heaviness (Isaiah 61:3).
- Spirit of harlotry (Hosea 5:4).
- Foul spirit (Mark 9:25).
- Deaf and dumb/mute spirit (Mark 9:17-29).
- Spirit of infirmity (Luke 13:10).
- Spirit of divination (Acts 16:16).
- Spirit of bondage (Romans 8:15).

- Spirit of the world (1 Corinthians 2:12).
- Spirit of death (1 Corinthians 10:10, 1 Corinthians 15:26).
- Seducing spirit (1 Timothy 4:1).
- Spirit of fear (2 Timothy 1:7).
- Spirit of antichrist (1 John 4:3).
- Spirit of error (1 John 4:6).[1]

The Devil wishes to deceive the true Church, by working through tares in the hope he can set up a counterfeit church, within the real, and outside of the real, that can be used to steal/poach real believers into and dampen their faith. This is the counterfeit bride which Jesus taught on, which Satan is raising up (Mark 13:22). This is an expression of female rebellion which will not submit to God, as John warned (Revelation 2:20, Revelation 17:1-18). It is the personification and embodiment of rebellion, by being wedded to the world, instead of Christ. This is a representation of wickedness, the unseen force in all the earth; which seeks ever to be hidden further and deeper away (Zechariah 5:5-9). These tares will fully embrace the Antichrist when he comes.

Paul does not teach that being a true member in Christ's Church will lead to a life of ease, because we are invited into a war, where we are to wrestle with evil spirits through prayer and intercession. 'For we do not wrestle against flesh and blood, but against principalities, against powers, against the rulers of the darkness of this age, against spiritual hosts of wickedness in the heavenly places' (Ephesians 6:12).

Tares are hosts of antichrist spirits here on earth, who have direct communication with spiritual hosts of wickedness in heavenly places. They are spiritual spies who inform the powers of darkness about believers that are serving the Lord, or about the wider work of the Body of Christ, through a faithful church and obedient ministry etc., which is a threat to Satan's kingdom (Matthew 25:41).

One way or another, tares are committed to bring division, but it is impossible to fight tares in the power of the flesh (2 Corinthians 10:3). The demons in them will do all they can, by any means, to provoke you to sin. 'And a servant of the Lord must not quarrel but be gentle to all, able to teach, patient' (2 Timothy 2:24). The true servant of the Lord must always operate in love, because God is sovereign; He is in control of all things and all things are under His control. As Jesus explained, God has allowed tares to be sown amongst His people and He told us that we too must be aware (Matthew 13:28-30). Consequently, do not be surprised if God allows a tare to continually provoke you, because it will produce in you the fruit of the Holy Spirit and will teach you additional lessons on spiritual warfare (2 Corinthians 12:7). When you come under attack by a tare, if you remain in Christ, abide in His love and walk in the light as He does, then you will be taken into greater paths of victory.

Be warned, a tare will go to any lengths necessary to gain victory over his or her prey. They are soul partners with Satan and his will. They are by nature two-faced, double-minded, and masters of deception. If called to, they will use their bodies to manipulate others into sin, those of the opposite sex, or those of the same sex – all to destroy God's work.

For the majority of Christians, spiritual warfare is a hidden mystery and so is any tare amongst them. It is the very nature of spiritual warfare to be clandestine. These tares are like obstinate children; stubborn, self-willed and unyielding. They like to form an alliance, but not by the Spirit of the Lord, as Isaiah declared (Isaiah 30:1). They are rebellious, deceitful and unwilling to listen to the Lord's instructions. They despise seers, prophets and visions, which God gives of what is right and holy, whilst they remain 'religious!' They want only to hear pleasant things, not the truth which they hate, because the Holy Spirit is shining a spotlight on them and their work, and they despise being confronted by the Holy Spirit.

As tares are sown into God's Kingdom and pretend to be true disciples of Jesus, they will generally honour God with their lips, but their hearts are far from Him (Isaiah 30:8-16, Jeremiah 3:10). They bring trouble on themselves by forsaking God and going after another, yet they believe that they have not sinned and done no wrong (Jeremiah 2:13, 19, 35). These tares desire the praise and approval of others, and will seek ways to get it, even through inordinate affections. They are driven from within and strive for acceptance, and believe that everyone has a price at which they can be bought, just as Judas, one of the Twelve Disciples was bought for thirty pieces of silver/thirty silver coins. They will go to great lengths over periods of time to ensnare others. They are often devoid of any peace and are tormented. They seek out the attention of others by doing good works for the Lord (Amos 5:21), purely to make themselves feel better and in a similar fashion to the Pharisees, to inwardly say, "Look at me," to get outward praise and public recognition (Matthew 6:5).

All true born-again Christian believers know that in repentance and rest, they will find the peace and joy of their salvation. In quietness and confidence will be their strength (Isaiah 30:15); but tares will have none of this. Tares will not surrender or accept defeat and the Body of Christ, the living Church needs to wake up to this fact, and deal with all that is demonic in their ranks (Ephesians 3:10).

A word of warning, do not overreact and begin a witch-hunt in the flesh, this is not being led of the Spirit. A true tare will be more than eager to assist you to wage war and bring false accusation against others, which will only add further confusion, paranoia and disunity.

The demons that ensnare a religious person to become a tare have had thousands of years to perfect their art of deception. Without the guidance of the Holy Spirit, who uncovers their deception, the Church is helpless. Tares are made up of a nest of demons that can vary considerably. Every nest will have a strong man or ruling spirit, a religious spirit and an antichrist spirit, including a host of others. Each nest is tailor-made to plant next to an individual who serves Christ, or a church, or a Bible College, or a ministry, to discourage, dissolve or destroy them/it. I repeat on purpose: they are well trained and are planted by demons that are of a higher order than they are. Jesus met a man who was possessed by a demonic strong man called Legion, and this strong man was in control of thousands of devils in this one man, enough to drive around two thousand pigs down a steep place, into the sea to their destruction! It said to Jesus, "My name is Legion, for we are many" (Mark 5:9).

Tares are a law unto themselves, as the apostles found (3 John 9-11). On the outside, because of their striving religious spirit they may appear at first, to be an answer to prayer because they are keen to be seen in the ministry of helps, yet for all the wrong reasons. They have perfected the image of servant-hood, with the purpose of getting into the inner circle, and into positions of influence or control. More often than not, they will go the extra mile, appearing considerate and are often the first to think of giving cards or presents to people, and taking an interest in others, to gain information.

To gain acceptance and mastery, they are so devious that they may continue unseen for years, working hard, contributing, whilst all the time the enemy is embedding them into the church, ministry, Bible College etc. for the right time of his choosing. Nevertheless, the true believers will discern that on the inside, they are rebels and always will be, and the prophets who speak up to warn of them must be heeded.

Just like spies during the Cold War period, these tares are like terrorist sleeper cells, waiting for years to be in the right place at the right time to undermine God's work. Like Islamic extremists, these people can appear to be just another friendly person, but suddenly they awake after years to cause havoc. Tares may be great tithers and even give offerings, they may teach or lead prayer groups, because they have learnt to be all things to all men – but they are big trouble!

The last thing we need right now are church buildings full of Christians who believe this, that and the other, yet never do anything – but meet regularly. What is required, are disciples of Jesus who adhere to the teaching of the Bible. Christians filled with the Holy Spirit and obedient to Him, operating in the gift of discernment, to see what the enemy is doing. With the coming of the Antichrist in the future, those without the Holy Spirit in their churches will be at the Devil's mercy, because he has no mercy, and they may even welcome him. Satan has already planted scoffers in churches, sent to undermine faith and belief in God's revelation for the last days (2 Peter 3:3).

As ever, to gain victory over tares, we must walk in the Holy Spirit, accept His gift of discernment and wisdom, and walk in God's love. The Holy Spirit taught me that we can only gain victory over tares by always operating in His love, then we can shut them up, shut them down and shut them out – ex-communication from God's work. Elisha the prophet knew how to deal with tares in God's house, as he would never look at them or notice them. Elisha said, "As the Lord of hosts lives, before whom I stand, surely were it not that I regard the presence of Jehoshaphat king of Judah, I would not look at you, nor see you" (2 Kings 3:14-15).

Chapter Seven

Spiritual Tarerorism (Terrorism)

God said to Jeremiah, "Even if Moses and Samuel stood before Me, My mind would not be favourable toward this people. Cast them out of My sight, and let them go forth" (Jeremiah 15:1).

Tares because of their own self-importance are more often than not, seeking attention one way or another. They are pre-programmed to put self first. The more time and attention you give to a tare, only tends to feed and empower the antichrist spirits in them. The tare misinterprets your actions and is emboldened to keep coming back for more. All the time and attention that a tare receives is perceived as acceptance as part of the Body of Christ, when they are not part of the Body of Christ, the Church. Scripture makes it very plain that tares and their behaviour have no part or place in the true Church.

Because of the ungodly traits of tares, it is imperative that you are led of the Holy Spirit and not your emotions – your feelings, which can be both powerful and misleading. Jesus always spoke the truth and faced others with it, and we must do the same. Jesus said, "If you abide in My word, you are My disciples indeed. And you shall know the truth, and the truth shall make you free" (John 8:31-32).

Tares commit spiritual tarerorism (terrorism). Their aim is to sabotage Kingdom work and all who are involved in it. To discourage, dishearten, to depress, to hinder, harass or harangue those who are active in advancing the Kingdom of God, especially those in Christian ministry.

We suffer what we tolerate. The Lord spoke to Moses, the leader of the nation of Israel, and said, "If you do not drive out the inhabitants of the land from before you, *then it shall be that those whom you let remain shall be irritants in your eyes and thorns in your sides, and they shall harass you in the land where you dwell"* (Numbers 33:55).

John Wesley, the founder of Methodism with his brother Charles, was greatly used during the British Great Awakening (1739-1791), also known as the Evangelical Revival. He was married after his revival ministry had been underway for twelve years. Church history records that his wife was nothing but a complete nuisance to him and his ministry – a hindrance to the furtherance of the gospel. In 1752, John Wesley married a widow of a London merchant, Mrs Vazeille, who had four children – she was of independent fortune and died in October 1781. For the first four years Mrs Wesley travelled with her husband, but her absurd jealousy acted like fuel to her violent temper. She would frequently intercept the letters of her husband and give them into the hands of his enemies; interpolating words to make them bear a bad construction, and publish them in the newspapers!

In 1758, Mrs Wesley left her husband vowing never to see him again, but she negated on her promise and John suffered more. In her fits of jealousy, Mrs Wesley would order a chaise and drive a hundred miles to see who was with her husband in his carriage when he entered town. On one occasion, one of Wesley's preachers recounted: 'John Hampton, told his son that he once went into a room in the north of Ireland, where he found Mrs Wesley foaming with rage. Her husband was on the floor. She had been dragging him about by his hair and still held in her hand some of the locks that she had pulled out of his head in fury!' John Wesley was only five feet in height and weighed under 126 lb / 57.15 kg. More than once she laid violent hands upon him and tore his venerable locks which had suffered sufficiently from the ravages of time.[1]

The job function of a tare in brief is to make the servants of the Lord's work and call as difficult as possible, through constant harassment, verbal or otherwise. Over long periods of time, it will be direct and indirect, openly and clandestine, by every plausible lie, deceit and deception. This is not uncommon; in the Bible there are many reference to false: teachers, preachers, prophets and apostles, as well as those who profess to be religious, yet have wicked, devious, corrupt or evil hearts. Many of these people profess to serve God, yet have been weighed in God's balance and been found wanting!

One of the most shocking accounts is the people at Jerusalem who were in gross idolatry in and around the temple of God. Ezekiel saw the abominations in a vision. Around the courtyard of the temple of God were idols and images, and they also adorned the inside of the temple, the most holiest place on earth in its time. Seventy of the elders of Israel, each had a censer in their hands and were committing rituals to these false gods and demonic deities. The women were weeping for the god Tammuz. At the door of the temple of the Lord were twenty-five men facing east, with their backs towards the temple of the Lord and they were worshipping the sun! (Ezekiel 8).

'The sacrifice of the wicked is an abomination; *how much more when he brings it with wicked intent!* A false witness shall perish, but the man who hears him will speak endlessly' (Proverbs 21:27-28).

The Lord speaking through John said, "To the angel of the church of Ephesus write: 'These things says He who holds the seven stars in His right hand, who walks in the midst of the seven golden lampstands, "I know your works, your labour, your patience, and that you cannot bear those who are evil. And *you have tested those who say they are apostles and are not, and have found them liars*" ' " (Revelation 2:1-2).

The Lord speaking through John said, "And to the angel of the church in Smyrna write: 'These things says the First and the Last, who was dead, and came to life, "I know your works, tribulation, and poverty (but you are rich); and *I know the blasphemy of those who say they are Jews and are not, but are a synagogue of Satan*" ' " (Revelation 2:8-9). C.f. Rev. 3:9.

To the churches at Ephesus and Smyrna, Jesus said, "I know." He knew what they were up to, who was present and who was good, bad or in error. Some said they were apostles but were found to be liars and some said they were Jews, but were a synagogue of Satan! Some people in churches say they are Christian, when they are not, they could be tares!

When dealing with a tare you are not dealing directly with a person, but a nest of demonic/evil spirits working through the tare. The Devil working through the demons through the tare who is completely deceived and deluded. Their behaviour will vary depending on your relationship to the tare such as: in a family, church, ministry, Bible College or Christian community.

When faced with the stiff-necked people of Judah and their worthless religion (because of their ungodly actions), the prophet Jeremiah was told by the Lord – not to pray for their wellbeing! (Jeremiah 14:11). 'Thus says the Lord to this people, "Thus they have loved to wander; they have not restrained their feet. Therefore the Lord does not accept them; He will remember their iniquity now, and punish their sins." Then the Lord said to me, "Do not pray for this people, for their good. When they fast, I will not hear their cry; and when they offer burnt offering and grain offering, I will not accept them. But I will consume them by the sword, by the famine, and by the pestilence" ' (Jeremiah 14:10-12).

God's righteous anger was so aroused over Judah's sin that He said to Jeremiah, "Even if Moses and Samuel stood before Me, My mind would not be favourable toward this people. Cast them out of My sight, and let them go forth." (Jeremiah 15:1). It is the same today, tares will be separated at the end of the age and are reserved for the judgment of God's fire (hell). Jesus said, "Therefore as the tares are gathered and burned in the fire, so it will be at the end of this age. The Son of Man will send out His angels, and they will gather *out of His Kingdom* all things that offend, and those who practice lawlessness, and will cast them into the furnace of fire. There will be wailing and gnashing of teeth. Then the righteous will shine forth as the sun in the Kingdom of their Father. He who has ears to hear, let him hear!" (Matthew 13:40-43). Therefore, it is pointless to pray for tares to change their ways. They have gone too far and are so deceived and deluded, that they cannot and will not change. God's good, pleasing and perfect will is that they be thrown into the fire by His angels.

God's judgment against rebellion is very real and final, from an individual tare, to a nation. There comes a time when enough is enough and no amount of prayer, fasting or intercession can change the course of events. God's mind is set and His righteous judgment will prevail. The word of the Lord to Ezekiel the prophet was, ' "Son of man, when a land sins against Me by persistent unfaithfulness, I will stretch out My hand against it; I will cut off its supply of bread, send famine on it, and cut off man and beast from it. Even if these three men, Noah, Daniel, and Job, were in it, they would deliver only themselves by their righteousness," says the Lord

God.' "...Even though Noah, Daniel, and Job were in it, as I live," says the Lord God, "they would deliver neither son nor daughter; they would deliver only themselves by their righteousness" (Ezekiel 14:13-14, 20).

Tares led on by demons will seek out and find ways or others to do all they can to discourage, dishearten and depress you through avenues of:

- Fear
- Anger
- Malice
- Gossip
- Judging
- Tension
- Belittling
- Violence
- Criticism
- Irritability
- Theatrics
- Rejection
- Suspicion
- Arguments
- Accusation
- Quarrelling
- Intolerance
- Intimidation
- Faultfinding
- Concealment
- Confrontation
- Annoying behaviour
- Antagonise and goad
- Anti-submissiveness etc.
- Vulnerability (they feign need for help).

This list is not exhaustive but gives a general guide as to the avenues of how a tare operates. Not all traits may be present and how a tare operates within a family, a church fellowship, ministry, Bible College/Seminary or Christian community can differ. All tares have rebellion towards God in their hearts and despise His servants; outwardly they may appear loving, but inside they are full of bitterness and demonic hatred. Some tares:

- If they cannot get their own way, they may sulk, have a tantrum or a rant; some lose all self-control. They cannot be reasoned with and a lot of what comes out of their mouth, they cannot recall ever saying! Then they ignore you and try to make you feel bad.
- Tares hate apologising, often they will not and after a period of ignoring you (because they could not get their own way), they pretend as if nothing has happened and all is ok.
- They may cause problems before you go on a ministry trip, whilst you are away or when you come back. They may even tell confidential: family, church, ministry or Bible College/Seminary issues to others!
- They often accuse people of doing certain things, which they themselves are guilty of doing. They like to cause mischief.
- A tare may or may not have mental health issues, but many of their actions point in this direction. Most tares refuse all offers of help; as far as they are concerned there is no issue; you have a problem, not them. Most tares are so bound by Satan, programmed to do his will that they cannot be helped, only separated at the end of the age. This is sad but true.
- Some tares are critical of people's dress, food, attitudes, lack of money etc. They like to talk about themselves, what they have done, how good they are, whilst putting others down.
- Many have inordinate affections, they like to be *seen* doing good works, giving, helping others, offering compliments etc. They do this to feel good about themselves and to receive acknowledgement and thanks. "Isn't he/she good" etc.
- A tare will often fane humility, but revel in the attention because of their pride. This humility is a false humility as the apostle Paul wrote about to the Colossian Church (Colossians 2:18), which was also to be circulated to the Laodicean Church (Colossians 4:16).
- A tare may appear vulnerable and in need of help, but can quickly sap the energy and strength from a leader (or others who are of a helping disposition), and begin to discourage members of the fellowship.

If a tare confronts you, any weakness you have will be tested to the full. To overcome and claim victory in Christ you must become an overcomer, walking in the light as He is the light (1 John 1:7). Walking in His love, which produces all the fruit of the Holy Spirit with a heart filled with mercy, compassion and forgiveness. This can only happen when you have crucified your flesh and are *truly filled* with the Holy Spirit.[2] (See chapter ten for more details about overcomers).

Remember, turning off the attention tap is like turning off oxygen to the lungs; shutting them out, shuts them up, which in turn shuts them down.

Warnings from Scripture

- 'Do not be carried about with various and strange doctrines...' (Hebrews 13:9).
- 'Even if we, or an angel from heaven preach any other gospel to you than what we have preached to you, let him be accursed' (Galatians 1:8).
- '...In latter times some will depart from the faith, giving heed to deceiving spirits and doctrines of demons' (1 Timothy 4:1).
- '...There will be false teachers among you, who secretly bring in destructive heresies...many will follow their destructive ways because of whom the way of truth will be blasphemed. By covetousness they will exploit you with deceptive words...and their destruction will not slumber' (2 Peter 2:1-3).
- 'For certain men have crept in unnoticed, who long ago were marked out for this condemnation, ungodly men, who turn the grace of God into licentiousness and deny the only Lord God and our Lord Jesus Christ' (Jude verse 4).
- The apostle Paul said to the Ephesians, "...After my departure savage wolves will come in among you, not sparing the flock. Also from among yourselves men will rise up, speaking perverse things, to draw away the disciples after themselves" (Acts 20:29-30).
- Jesus said, "Not everyone who says to Me 'Lord, Lord,' shall enter the Kingdom of heaven, but he who does the will of My Father in heaven" (Matthew 7:21).

Chapter Eight

Dealing with Tares

'All Scripture is given by inspiration of God, and is profitable for doctrine, for reproof, for correction, for instruction in righteousness, that the man of God may be complete, thoroughly equipped for every good work' (2 Timothy 3:16-17).

The purpose of dealing with tares in your midst is to weaken, minimise and to neutralise the negative influence they can have on a church, Bible College/Seminary or Christian ministry etc., so they can no longer have a negative impact. Frequently there might only be a single tare who may try to groom others into his or her fold and the unwitting people can become the children/disciples of a tare. The tare has made a counterfeit disciple and the unknowing or the unwitting person has submitted themselves to the tare, and thus comes into alignment with the Devil and his plans. The counterfeit disciple of the tare can go from bad to worse as he or she begins to reflect and imitate the tare and thus becomes a tare in his or her own right. A tare in the process of grooming may be the leader of a clique but often only grooms one person at a time. The tare can focus better when he or she gives fully of him or herself to one person to lure them into his or her fold, but may prefer others to be around to help empower and bolster him or her. The leaders of some cliques are often rebellious or snobbish (and not necessarily tares), because they prefer the company of like-minded people, often along social or economical lines of the haves versus the have-nots.

Dealing with a tare is usually done in stages and often the tare knows that his or her work is at an end in a church, Bible College or Christian ministry etc. and will want to leave. However, this is not always the case, as the aim of a tare is to be in control and to hinder the work of the Kingdom of God. A tare is most effective in their devious dealings when he or she is in a position of leadership or trust and will not give up, surrender or relinquish, their role without a struggle or a fight.

Dealing with tares is not a straightforward issue, but biblical and spiritual rules *must* apply and be adhered to if you have any hope in gaining the victory and maintaining the high ground. You are not fighting against flesh and blood, but principalities and powers. The strong man must be bound, you must walk in the Spirit and be led of the Spirit; with a Kingdom mindset, having the mind of Christ, moving in love, doing all for the glory of God and exhibiting the fruit of the Spirit. You must not quarrel, intimidate, dominate, manipulate, be provoked to anger or do anything in the flesh. We are called to be submissive to those who are in authority over us and to pray spiritual prayers (those guided by the Holy Spirit) and not just our whims or desires, which may be soulish prayers, which can have their roots in demonic or fleshly wisdom and can cause chaos in the spiritual realm, in the heavenlies (James 3:14-15, James 4:1-3).

How a pastor deals with a tare in his congregation is different than how a member of the congregation would (or could), if he or she found out that someone in a position of leadership is a tare! A conundrum is, if a leader (or your superior) is a tare, how can you submit to them (in relation to biblical headship) when they are doing the work of the enemy? Other questions have to be posed: What are you doing in that church, chapel or denomination? Has the Holy Spirit called you to that church etc., or did you make that choice yourself? To be led of the Spirit is to be directed by the Spirit, and that includes your place of worship, or the denomination that you may or may not be a part of or joined in membership to. One man who had been to Bible College was desperate to become a member of a particular church denomination, but on a local level the church denied some fundamental doctrines which the man had experienced. As it was pointed out to him, when he sought advice, either you deny what is in the Bible and the biblical experiences you have, or renounce them (which means throwing away your Bible), and apply for local church membership! The man could not throw away his Bible, he loved the Word of God and was sorely torn between the two.

Tares (or weeds) can only be separated at the end of the age and so they must grow together with the wheat until that time. This does not mean that you have to suffer them or be tormented by them, because you don't. However, it does reveal the delicate nature of dealing with tares because if you try to pull up a tear by hand (working in the flesh), you will also disturb and uproot some wheat.

For those in leadership, you cannot really say to someone, "You are a tare." They won't believe it and it would probably make matters worse. You could be wrong in your spiritual diagnosis and could greatly hinder the person's future walk with the Lord. They may have issues in their life (most people have issues to be worked through), perhaps they need deliverance, they could be young in the Lord, immature or have little working knowledge of the Bible. It does take time to grow in the grace of God and to have one's mind renewed.

If they have come out from a cult or another religion, the undoing process of false teaching and error could take months or years to be corrected. They will certainly need deliverance from deceiving spirits and doctrines of demons (1 Timothy 4:1). People who have suffered trauma or abuse at the hands of perpetrators need time for issues to be resolved. To walk in with size 12 boots, stamp the ground and say, "You are a tare!" is simply wrong, unwise and foolish. If someone is causing untold problems, he or she may be doing the work of a tare and you may, after prayer, and having spoken to the person about the issues on more than a few occasions, feel that it is acceptable to say in gentleness and love, "You are doing the work of a tare."

I have known people in Christian ministry who truly love the Lord, but because they have never *fully* surrendered themselves to the Lord, they are not led of the Spirit, and so some of their actions have the hallmarks of a tare. They have caused major problems for others in ministry, but I could not say they are tares, but were working in the flesh.

The following is *general* guidelines and suggestions. Each tare is different and how a tare works can change and morph, just like a computer virus with mutating algorithms; you think you have the solution and then it changes to defend itself and its position.

Every person who has to deal with a tare should seek the Holy Spirit for His guidance *to know exactly* what they should do, and how to go about it. You should consider prayer and fasting to tune your spiritual receptors. To bring you into being one in truth and spirit with the Holy Spirit, and continue to abide in Jesus, the true Vine. You may not feel able to fast for an entire day, but you may be able to eat one meal a day for x amount of days, perhaps two weeks, a month or forty days. You should not go looking for tares, in search of trouble and remember, it is not a witch-hunt! You should always operate in love, walking in the Spirit and not in the flesh.

Jesus said, "The Kingdom of heaven is like a man who sowed good seed in his field; but while men slept, his enemy came and sowed tares among the wheat and went his way. But when the grain had sprouted and produced a crop, then the tares also appeared." So the servants of the owner came and said to him, 'Sir, did you not sow good seed in your field? How then does it have tares?' He said to them, 'An enemy has done this.' The servants said to him, *'Do you want us then to go and gather them up?'* But he said, 'No, lest while you gather up the tares you also uproot the wheat with them. Let both grow together until the harvest, and at the time of harvest I will say to the reapers, "First gather together the tares and bind them in bundles to burn them, but gather the wheat into my barn" ' " (Matthew 13:24-30).

Notice the delicate and sensitive matter of dealing with tares, 'Do you want us then to go and gather them up?' But he said, 'No, lest while you gather up the tares you also uproot the wheat with them' (verses 28-29). You do no want to uproot the wheat (true believers) or to cause them to stumble. If you come in hard, working in the flesh, trying to deal with a tare, other believers who are unaware of the situation (who and what the person is – a tare), may become unsettled in their faith and it could become a stumbling block for them. Dealing with a tare has to be done in a certain way and that involves spiritual warfare. You cannot work in the flesh or take a rod to them! You have to operate in love, in the Spirit and adhere to biblical principles and rules for spiritual warfare.

Scriptures to Remember

- Have a Kingdom mindset, put God first. Jesus said, "Seek first the Kingdom of God and His righteousness..." (Matthew 6:33a). Jesus said, "No one, having put his hand to the plow, and looking back, is fit for the Kingdom of God" (Luke 9:62).

- Have the mind of Christ and apply it. 'For what man knows the things of a man except the spirit of the man which is in him? Even so no one knows the things of God except the Spirit of God. Now we have received, not the spirit of the world, but the Spirit who is from God, that we might know the things that have been freely given to us by God. These things we also speak, not in words which man's wisdom teaches but which the Holy Spirit teaches, comparing spiritual things with spiritual. But the natural man does not receive the things of the Spirit of God, for they are foolishness to him; nor can he know them, because they are spiritually discerned. But he who is spiritual judges all things, yet he himself is rightly judged by no one. For...we have the mind of Christ' (1 Corinthians 2:11-16b).

- Be filled and led by the Spirit. Be 'filled with the Spirit' (Ephesians 5:18), 'walk in the Spirit' (Galatians 5:16-18, 25), and be 'led of the Spirit' (Romans 8:14).

- Do everything in love. 'Love suffers long and is kind; love does not envy; love does not parade itself, is not puffed up; does not behave rudely, does not seek its own, is not provoked, thinks no evil; does not rejoice in iniquity, but rejoices in the truth; bears all things, believes all things, hopes all things, endures all things. Love never fails...' (1 Corinthians 13:4-8a).

- Do all for the glory of God. 'Therefore, whether you eat or drink, or whatever you do, do all to the glory of God' (1 Corinthians 10:31).

- Exhibit the fruit of the Spirit. 'But the fruit of the Spirit is love, joy, peace, longsuffering, kindness, goodness, faithfulness, gentleness, self-control. Against such there is no law' (Galatians 5:22-23).

- You are not fighting against flesh and blood, but principalities and powers. 'For we do not wrestle against flesh and blood, but against principalities, against powers, against the rulers of the darkness of this age, against spiritual hosts of wickedness in the heavenly places' (Ephesians 6:12).

- Bind the strong man in the name of Jesus Christ. Jesus said, "How can one enter a strong man's house and plunder his goods, unless he first binds the strong man? And then he will plunder his house. He who is not with Me is against Me, and he who does not gather with Me scatters abroad" (Matthew 12:29-30). See also Matthew 16:19, Matthew 18:18-20, Mark 3:27 and Luke 11:21-23.
- 'And a servant of the Lord must not quarrel but be gentle to all, able to teach, patient' (2 Timothy 2:24).

For those in positions of leadership, the rules for deacons and elders, or how to handle contentions, those who are in sin, causing problems, those in opposition, the lazy/idle, gossipers, busybodies etc. are clearly laid down by Paul's letters and his pastoral epistles. They should be read and studied time and time again, not only by those in leadership, but by all Christians. Perhaps half the problems of pastors could be resolved if members of their congregations adhered to what the Bible says. 'Be doers of the Word' (James 1:22a).

To reiterate, the following is *general* guidelines and suggestions. Each person who has to deal with a tare, should walk in love and be led of the Holy Spirit – you dare not forget this. Each of the Scriptures on the previous pages must be adhered to and applied in each case. Remember, you should not say to someone, "You are a tare!" In each case, the strong man must be bound in Jesus' mighty name, during daily prayer. To bind the strong man, the spirit of the antichrist in (e.g. John or Jane) is to weaken their power and influence (Luke 10:18-19, Romans 16:20. 1 John 4:4). Then you must pray that God's good, perfect and pleasing will be done in this situation (Luke 11:2, Romans 12:2). Throughout you can ask the Holy Spirit, what are you trying to teach me through this? Ask the Holy Spirit how best to pray in each situation when dealing with a tare.

The following is a model prayer: "Heavenly Father, I (or we) come in the name of our Lord and Saviour Jesus Christ and I bind the strong man, the spirit of the antichrist, that controls the tare. And I ask for Your good, pleasing and perfect will in this situation, in Jesus' name I ask, amen."

'Therefore I exhort first of all that supplications, prayers, intercessions, and giving of thanks be made for all men, for kings and all who are in authority, that we may lead a quiet and peaceable life in all godliness and reverence' (1 Timothy 2:1-2).

A Church Member who is a Tare

Do not let them feed off you and sap your energy or time. Spiritual prescriptions are excellent aids to keep people who waste your time at bay. They may have to read a certain book of the Bible or a chapter of Proverbs a day; go make amends/restitution. A spiritual prescription is a way to help the person in his or her Christian walk, and to determine if he or she is serious or not. A person may question, why should I submit to those in authority? You can write out the relevant Scripture verses for them to look up (or dictate them), e.g. 1 Corinthians 16:15-16, Ephesians 5:21-28, Colossians 3:18-24, James 3:7, 1 Peter 2:13-25, 1 Peter 5:1-9 etc. Tell them to study the verses at home, and you will discuss it with them the following week. If they turn up the following week and have not done what you asked them to do, then it is a good indication that they are not serious. There may be a good reason, their child has been taken into hospital, a death in the family etc. They may ask a vexing question and you have a Christian book that covers that particular issue. You loan them the book and agree to meet them again in two to four weeks, when they should have finished the book. If they turn up and have not read the book, e.g. "I got bored after the second chapter," then the vexing question could not have been that vexing after all, otherwise they would have read the book and found the answers. If they have not fulfilled their obligations, you are under no duty to help them because they cannot be serious. Jesus said to the man at the pool of Bethesda, "Do you want to be made well?" (John 5:2-7).

Be cautious that the tare in your congregation does not try and lure others into their lair/under his or her wings. Do not give them positions of influence or authority within your church. This includes being part of the worship team, serving tea, cleaning the church/chapel, leading or heading up any groups. Do not give them an opportunity to preach, or ask them by name to pray publicly. Do not give them a set of keys to the church building or out buildings.

When it comes to dealing with a tare, in all probability it will go on and on for months, if not years. But at every stage, those in leadership must keep their God-given authority and take control of the process, and not allow the tare to think or believe that he or she is in control. Those in leadership, especially teachers, will receive a stricter judgment (James 3:1), and will have a higher accountability, as those who have been entrusted with much (Luke 12:48, 1 Thessalonians 2:4). Those in leadership positions must protect the flock of whom God has made them overseers (Acts 20:28, 1 Peter 5:1-4).

An Elder or Deacon who is a Tare

If an elder or a deacon is a tare, then it is best to try and remove that person from his or her position of authority or service. This is easier said than done, and denominations may have their own rules and regulations which have to be adhered to. Some leadership roles run for x amount of years before the next vote. Do not tell tares anything confidential. Do not allow them to lay hands on anyone in prayer (this is easier said than done). If possible remove the opportunities for a tare to preach, teach or pray in public. If you have an open time of prayer, you cannot ask them not to pray, or to stop praying. However, as a pastor you should *not* ask them to pray over the offering, before Communion, at the close of the service etc. By exclusion, you can begin to shut them down; this is not being mean or vindictive, but is spiritual warfare. Leaders have to protect the flock of whom God has made them overseers.

A Tare in your Ministry

Following all of the previous advice under A Church Member who is a Tare and An Elder or a Deacon who is a Tare. Once again, a lot of the following is easier said than done. If you have a tare in your ministry, can he or she be made redundant, let go, or are they on a short-term contract, which will soon expire. Employment laws and tribunals are tricky, costly and reflect badly on Christian ministries. You cannot really sack/fire someone when outwardly he or she is doing their job correctly. Even if you were to say in love, "You are doing the work of a tare," (*not* you are a tare), the person would deny this accusation, because the tare would not even know it.

Tares are deceived, yet sincerely believe that they are doing the work of the Lord, whilst they may be praying, unbeknown to you, against the ministry and its leadership.

If you are having a few doubts about dealing with a tare, then the following testimony may be of help. I too was once in a similar situation with doubts and concerns regarding a tare, but I had to face the facts that were presented to me. I was the leader of a small church which had been meeting for many years. One person who joined us at the beginning was often troublesome, but refused all offers of help and practical ministry/deliverance. We had a real problem, and every time I sought the Holy Spirit to know how best to deal with the situation, I was forced to consider that this person was a tare. At the same time, my mind was bombarded with fear and doubt. One day, in desperation, I pleaded with the Holy Spirit to speak to me in such a way that I could truly understand. The next Sunday, I was approached by the troublesome member whom I reluctantly believed was a tare. With a polite smile, I was informed that in my absence, there had been a church meeting where it had been unanimously agreed that I was to hand over the leadership and leave! I stated that if this was the case, then all members of the church should meet to discuss the reasons for their actions. I was firmly informed that this was not necessary, as the entire group had already decided. However, I insisted. It transpired that no meeting had taken place and the group were aghast at such a suggestion. The tare still insisted that the group had met, yet different members openly said, "No we did not." The tare left the church and later wormed its way into another fellowship. I was informed some time afterwards that within weeks of joining the new fellowship, the tare volunteered to help in any way the person could and was accepted into different areas of church ministry!

Jesus said, "If you abide in My Word, you are My disciples indeed. And you shall know the truth, and the truth shall make you free" (John 8:31-32).

Chapter Nine

Beware of the Visit-Tare (Visiting Tare)

'Now David was sitting between the two gates. And the watchman went up to the roof over the gate, to the wall, lifted his eyes and looked, and there was a man, *running alone*' (2 Samuel 18:24).

Thomas Phillips documented the 1859 Welsh Revival. In his rebuttal to the objections that the new converts will backslide, betray religion and bring disgrace on the whole movement, he wrote: 'Suppose this would be found true in part, where would be the marvel? Is not the Kingdom of heaven compared to ten virgins, of whom five were foolish? And to a net cast into the sea, which gathered of every kind? And is not the Christian Church a field in which wheat and tares grow together until harvest? We must be prepared for disappointments – a Judas will appear here – a Demas there – Simon the sorcerer, Diotrephes, and men of kindred spirit will "arise" again. It has been so in former revivals.... Have we right to expect that the present will be an exception!?'

'Then Jesus sent the multitude away and went into the house. And His disciples came to Him, saying, "Explain to us the parable of the tares of the field." He answered and said to them, "He who sows the good seed is the Son of Man. The field is the world, the good seeds are the sons of the Kingdom, but the tares are the sons of the wicked one. The enemy who sowed them is the Devil, the harvest is the end of the age and the reapers are the angels. Therefore as the tares are gathered and burned in the fire, so it will be at the end of this age. The Son of Man will send out His angels, and they will gather out of His Kingdom all things that offend, and those who practice lawlessness, and will cast them into the furnace of fire. There will be wailing and gnashing of teeth. Then the righteous will shine forth as the sun in the Kingdom of their

Father. He who has ears to hear, let him hear!" ' (Matthew 13:36-43).

There is a truth that Christians in most denominations are agreed upon, that we are living in the last days, the end times (Matthew 24, Mark 13, Luke 21). When it comes to tares, it is a very different story. In all my years, outside of my own Christian walk and ministry, I can only recall once hearing a pastor mentioning a tare. With the last days comes the end time harvest, with the sons of the Kingdom growing alongside the sons of the evil one, as Scripture states. Jesus made it very plain in this parable (Matthew 13), that there will be an end time harvest, and with it, the end of the age, when Jesus will send out the angels to separate the good from the evil, and "they will gather out of His Kingdom" all things that offend (Matthew 13:41).

While large sections of the Church have been sleeping in the dark with their eyes closed, the Devil has sown his tares. The tares are ready and waiting for the next spiritual awakening, a heaven-sent revival when the Holy Spirit will come upon a dead Church and revive it. The Devil, anticipating this move of God, has already planted many of his tares, who will rise up and oppose the work of the Holy Spirit at this time, see Appendix A. So like watchman on the city walls, be on your guard and on the lookout for the visit-tare, 'Now David was sitting between the two gates. And the watchman went up to the roof over the gate, to the wall, lifted his eyes and looked, and there was a man, *running alone*' (2 Samuel 18:24). The visit-tare is a tare that drops in as a visitor on a dead or dying church, to be used by Satan to destroy it. In all probability, this church will have already had a visit by the Holy Spirit, in the body of an overcomer, who was sent to show them God's plan for them. The overcomers are covered in the next chapter.

God's plan for all churches has already been revealed. Plan A, is the narrow path that leads to the resurrection life in Christ Jesus (John 10:10, Acts 1:8), to be conformed into His image (Romans 8:29), to accomplish His mission – wrestling principalities and powers (Ephesians 3:10-11), and fulfilling the Great Commission (Mark 16:15). However, if they have already rejected the true light of His Word and the work of the Holy Spirit, then they have been made ready, by lying, deceiving spirits, to embrace the deception of the wide path that leads to destruction (1 Timothy 4:1). You have been warned. You will suffer what you tolerate.

At one time the Holy Spirit led me into a dead and dying church that was tucked away down a backstreet. When the congregation and the pastor expressed they had no desire for the Holy Spirit's power working there, He departed and instructed me to leave also. But waiting in the wings was a tare that the Devil had planted. When the pastor retired, the tare came forward and offered 'to help,' in any way the person could, and within a few months, all the leadership team had become subservient to the will of this tare! Even future pastors could do nothing without this person's approval! To the undiscerning visitor today, it is just another church struggling to stay alive. To the discerning, it is a counterfeit body, without the Holy Spirit and is dead.

As I have said before, remove a man's spirit and his body dies, remove the Holy Spirit from the Body of Christ, the Church and it dies also. You can keep a human body on a life-support machine for years and it looks as if the person is sleeping. It's the same with a dead church, you can keep it going, aided by money and give it the appearance of life, but in truth, it is already dead. Nobody wants to pull the plug on a life-support machine, but the Devil, working through a principality, working through tares, are more than happy to counterfeit the appearance of life, through a dead church fellowship. This false church will lead many to a lost eternity and stop others from entering into God's good, pleasing and perfect will for their lives, which is to be conformed into the image of His Son Jesus (Romans 8:29). The will of God for His Church is for it to have His life in them, in all its abundance (John 10:10), by the power of the Holy Spirit living in them (Acts 1:8, Acts 10:38). The tare wants to control all and resist the will of God the Holy Spirit; this leads us to the Jezebel spirit.

From the outset, let me make it plain. The Jezebel spirit is a spirit without gender and will target any willing man or woman to work through. The Jezebel spirit is a principality that operates through witchcraft, in the form of intimidation, manipulation and domination; aided by spirits of lies, deceit and deception. Jezebel is an unseen enemy, which influences every demon that works in and through tares. It has a true hatred of God-given male authority and hates prophets, intercessors, overcomers, and all the true servants of the Lord, with a passion unknown by most Christians.

Principalities are spiritual forces of evil, having strongholds over nations, people groups or geographical areas etc. These evil spirits are invisible to the human eye and can only be seen when you are 'in the Spirit' (Ezekiel 3:14, Ezekiel 37:1, Revelation 1:10). Such times are few and far between, and only comes to pass as the Holy Spirit wills. Therefore, it has pleased the Lord to use others on the earth at different times, to give us all an insight to the true nature of that spirit, which gives us a better understanding of how they operate, see 1 Kings 18:13-19, 1 Kings 21:5-11, 2 Kings 9:7, 22 and Revelation 2:20-24.

Tares, the demons in them and all controlling spirits over them must all be confronted and overcome by the Church (Ephesians 3:10-11). This was the pattern of the Lord Jesus and His disciples. 'Then the seventy returned with joy, saying, "Lord, even the demons are subject to us in Your name." And He said to them, "I saw Satan fall like lightning from heaven. Behold, I give you the authority to trample on serpents and scorpions, and over all the power of the enemy, and nothing shall by any means hurt you. Nevertheless do not rejoice in this, that the spirits are subject to you, but rather rejoice because your names are written in heaven" ' (Luke 10:17-20). For further study on the role of the Church binding, defeating and overcoming principalities and powers, see also Matthew 18:18-20, Colossians 2:9-15, James 2:17-19 and Revelation 12:10-11. For a greater understanding of Jesus' words, "I give you the authority to trample on serpents and scorpions" (Luke 10:19), see Job 26:13b, Psalm 91:13, Mark 16:18 and Acts 28:3-5.

When first confronted, a tare will more often than not, take a submissive stance, exhibiting an appearance of genuine concern for any misunderstandings (Acts 8:18-24). However, it will be only a matter of time, when the tare will have to be challenged by those in a position of authority over them (3 John 9-11). *Then* you will begin to experience the full force of the Jezebel spirit against you.

The principality Jezebel will control, manipulate, intimidate and dominate all the demons that make up the demonic nest in the tare. It will terrorise them (oppress by fear), to bring about its own counterfeit wicked will, by doing all they can to control, or destroy the person or the ministry of those it preys on. Tares are tormented to achieve their goal and hate true repentance, for they know it is the golden key to true freedom.

Be warned, when you declare war on tares, Jezebel will declare war on you, and you will discover some of your friends, family, and brethren alike, will begin to turn against you, and oppose you (1 Kings 19:1-4). However, you must stand firm in the full armour of God, with the Holy Spirit, in the name of Jesus Christ, washed in His blood and gain the victory over all your foes. Further warnings, you cannot live an unholy life and war against the Devil's demonic hordes. Do not go beyond your remit, your God-given authority; be led by the Holy Spirit at all times, and at every stage of the warfare.

A word of warning in your enthusiasm to defeat the enemy. Do not rush in – to attempt to bind some principality or power and pull down its stronghold without the clear leading of the Holy Spirit and His designated authority to do so, which is very rare in truth, much rarer than many believers might think.

Authority in spiritual warfare is gained by a good knowledge of the Holy Scriptures, through the Holy Spirit, through holy living and practical experience gained over time. You may read a book on spiritual warfare and have a head full of knowledge, but without any practical experience, you will be very vulnerable to a backlash of attacks (sudden and adverse). If you are truly led by the Holy Spirit to take a special interest in spiritual warfare, then the principalities and powers of darkness will take a special interest in you. Spiritual warfare is not for the faint or half-hearted or double-minded (Acts 19:15).

In the days that we live in, we come across more and more individuals who believe what they want to believe, they believe what they are comfortable with, or believe in half-truths; when quite clearly (to many others), they believe in the wrong half! Through no fault of their own, they were encouraged to pray a prayer of commitment to Christ, but have not *truly* repented of their sins, (and forsaken them) or turned away from their old lifestyles, and most have no intention of doing so (Matthew 7:23). They are not truly born-again, they do not have the Holy Spirit living in them, they have not passed from death to life.

Some of them who are bound by demonic strongholds have not received deliverance, and most have only a very basic knowledge of the Bible – they are biblically illiterate. Yet, they have been taken into church membership and are prime targets to be taken in and turned into tares (or lured into a cult).

As a deacon, I was attending a church meeting to discuss a maintenance project which would benefit our congregation. This would mean a considerable investment. I had attended this place of worship for several years and was surprised when a man that I had never seen or met before kept interrupting those who were sharing about the benefits of such a project. He became more and more opposed to the idea. Eventually, I rose to my feet and challenged him as to what right did he have to have an opinion on the matter? I was shocked to find out that he was a member! However, I pointed out to him that as he had not attended a single service in over two years, and did not financially contribute to the church, he should sit down and remain silent, which he did. This man was a tare. It turned out he would turn up from time to time and cause trouble.

What about Simon, the former sorcerer who was 'saved' during the revival at Samaria? Under the ministry of Phillip the evangelist, Simon believed in Jesus Christ, was baptised by Phillip and followed him, being amazed at the miracles and signs that were manifested under the ministry of anointed Phillip (Acts 8:5-13). Peter and John, the apostles from Jerusalem, heard of the great work in Samaria and went to them so that the brethren in Samaria might receive the Holy Spirit. Simon saw that the Holy Spirit could be imparted by the laying on of hands and wanted to buy this gift! Peter rebuked him, "Your money perish with you, because you thought that the gift of God could be purchased with money! You have neither part nor portion in this matter, for your heart is not right in the sight of God. Repent therefore of this your wickedness, and pray God if perhaps the thought of your heart may be forgiven you. For I see that you are poisoned by bitterness and bound by iniquity" (Acts 8:18-24).

To the countless number of hard-working, faithful pastors and ministers who are kept so busy to notice everything going on in their fellowship and have no wish to add another burden to their already overburdened list of things to do, this is one thing you *dare not ignore or brush aside* (Jonah 1:6, Romans 13:11-12). Why? Because Jesus spoke about it and explained it in the simplest way, through a parable. Would you ignore a cancerous growth in your own body? Of course not. So why ignore one in the Body of Christ? (2 Corinthians 6:15). You must act early to have any real chance of victory, with limited loss or damage to the flock. Every church fellowship will be visited by a wolf in sheep's clothing and if the watchman is not standing in the gap, and watching over the flock, they will be in peril.

The 1960s saw the beginning of the Charismatic Renewal with the Holy Spirit and His gifts being welcomed and embraced in multitudes of fellowships across the decades. However, other fellowships rejected the Holy Spirit or forbade Him to move in their midst. Church members who had been touched by the Holy Spirit were often told to keep quiet or to move on, to leave, and so many new fellowships came into being with like-minded people coming together. For others, the newfound freedom in the Spirit, could not be contained in some mainline church denominations at that time. With this fresh zeal and boldness, many believers became nomadic in their search for more of God and the reality of His power as revealed in the book of Acts. With this mass Christian migration of the old and new, coupled with different traditions and styles of church worship and leadership, there came the inevitable difficulties as the spiritual appetites and palates of believers varied greatly. Into this mix also came the seeds of discord, as the Devil exploited those who had issues in their lives. The germs of tares/weeds had been planted, which for some would lead to division and church splits, sometimes over the most trivial of things. This was due in part to the work of tares who are now well-rooted and waiting for the next true move of God.

A pastor shared how one Sunday morning his congregation doubled in size – real numerical growth. Many would have viewed this as an amazing answer to prayer. However, all was not as it seemed. The pastor was well-known in his community and he knew all the other fellowships in his area and their leaders. This addition to his congregation was born out of a church split, where often rebellion, unresolved issues and un-

Christian behaviour are at the fore. The pastor welcomed the new visitors and at the end of the meeting, with great wisdom, asked the new group to stay behind. He told them they were most welcome to attend his church, but he did not want them bringing in their old baggage connected with the church split. He did not want a church within a church and each person needed to deal with the past in forgiveness etc. before moving on into any new fellowship. The following week the congregation was back to its normal size.

Some years ago I was part of a Pentecostal Church when two women in their early thirties came for the first time. The pastor's wife made them feel most welcomed and the deacon served them communion. After the two women left, I shared with the pastor and his wife that the two visitors were Satanists. The pastor's wife was very upset, defensive and could not accept that they had been deceived. I suggested that if the women returned next week, they should be asked for their names and what church they last supported. The following Sunday, the women returned and the pastor's wife asked them their names etc. Without saying a word, they turned their backs and walked out!

You may not have a group come to your fellowship from a church split, or Satanists, but what about the person who has been caught in sin (e.g. adultery, theft, malicious backbiting etc.) and is unrepentant? The person has committed sin, he or she continues in sin and revels/enjoys their sinful lifestyle. The pastor or church elders have spoken to the guilty person and told him or her to repent and forsake their sin, but he or she refuses. The person's church membership has been revoked; if they were in leadership (or in any position of authority), he or she has had to step down. The person then turns up at your church, do you make inquiries and ask them about his or her Christian walk with the Lord and which church they have come from? If you discern something is not quite right, do you make further inquiries and speak to his or her former pastor? When the facts are known, should the person be embraced with open arms or told to repent and to be Christ-like in attitude and character? Christians make mistakes, but it is not biblical to embrace those who deliberately, habitually and wilfully ignore the Word of God and break His commands. Remember: 'A little leaven leavens the whole lump' (Galatians 5:9). 'Do you not know that a little leaven leavens the whole lump?' (1 Corinthians 5:6). 'Therefore let us keep the feast, not with old leaven, nor with the leaven of malice and wickedness, but with the unleavened bread of sincerity and truth' (1 Corinthians 5:8). God does require an account of that which is past (Ecclesiastes 3:15b), and unless we deal with the past, we cannot move forward into all that God has for us. It only took one person, Achan, to cause problems for the entire nation of Israel (Joshua 7).

The Great Commission must be fulfilled and one of the Church's job functions is to send forth more labourers into the harvest field (in prayer, financially and with people), to see the unreached reached; from every tribe, nation and tongue, coming to Jesus Christ and living for Him. If you allow trouble to abide in your midst, this will hinder the work. We are in a war (Revelation 12:17), but we stand on the side of victory, so take up the sword of the Spirit, the Word of God, and fight as the Holy Spirit directs. We must all give, go, pray and intercede as the Spirit leads, to glorify Jesus Christ to fulfil the great commission.

Some people may appear to be doing the work of a tare, but they may just need ministry, deliverance from demons. On the other hand it could be: immaturity, insecurity or a personality clash, where one or both parties have not crucified the flesh with its passions and desires and so one or both people could be at loggerheads with each other.

The question is posed: "How can I prevent myself from being deceived?" Because Jesus said, "Take heed that you do not be deceived..." (Luke 21:8). We should dig deep from the Word of God and have firm solid foundations in sound biblical doctrine. Most people do not decide to be deceived (or to deceive others), but it is a process that happens over time, a gradual process, rather than a sudden single event. We must all take heed as to who or what we are listening to, and who or what is influencing our knowledge of God and Christianity. We are all called to intelligently judge the message we hear and the person who brings it. For Christians, only the Holy Bible (God's objective Word) can truly judge our personal experiences (subjective feelings), thoughts, attitudes, doctrine and interpretation of Scripture, along with any preconceived ideas. 'What does the Scripture say?...' (Galatians 4:30a).

Chapter Ten

The Overcomers

'For whatever is born of God overcomes the world. And this is the victory that has overcome the world – our faith. Who is he who overcomes the world, but he who believes that Jesus is the Son of God?' (1 John 5:4-5).

Out of all the people that the Lord God led out of Egypt, who were twenty years old or above, only two crossed the Jordan River into the Promised Land. Why? Because they had a different spirit from the rest (Numbers 14:24). The Lord said, "Surely none of the men who came up from Egypt, from twenty years old and above, shall see the land of which I swore to Abraham, Isaac, and Jacob, because they have not wholly followed Me, except Caleb the son of Jephunneh, the Kenizzite, and Joshua the son of Nun, for they have wholeheartedly followed the Lord" (Numbers 32:11-13).

As recorded in the book of Revelation, Jesus spoke to the seven churches in Asia Minor. Whether positive or negative things were said, each Church had reference to him 'who overcomes' – the overcomers.

- To the Church at Ephesus, Jesus said, "He who has an ear, let him hear what the Spirit says to the churches. To him who *overcomes* I will give to eat from the tree of life, which is in the midst of the Paradise of God" (Revelation 2:7).

- To the Church at Smyrna, Jesus said, "He who has an ear, let him hear what the Spirit says to the churches. He who *overcomes* shall not be hurt by the second death" (Revelation 2:11).

- To the Church at Pergamos, Jesus said, "He who has an ear, let him hear what the Spirit says to the churches. To him who *overcomes* I will give some of the hidden manna to eat. And I will give him a white stone, and on the stone a new name written which no one knows except him who receives it" (Revelation 2:17).

- To the Church at Thyatira, Jesus said, "And he who *overcomes*, and keeps My works until the end, to him I will give power over the nations" (Revelation 2:26).

- To the Church at Sardis, Jesus said, "He who *overcomes* shall be clothed in white garments, and I will not blot out his name from the Book of Life; but I will confess his name before My Father and before His angels" (Revelation 3:5).

- To the Church at Philadelphia, Jesus said, "He who *overcomes*, I will make him a pillar in the temple of My God, and he shall go out no more. I will write on him the name of My God and the name of the city of My God, the New Jerusalem, which comes down out of heaven from My God. And I will write on him My new name" (Revelation 3:12).

- To the Church at Laodicea, Jesus said, "To him who *overcomes* I will grant to sit with Me on My throne, as I also overcame and sat down with My Father on His throne" (Revelation 3:21).

God said, "He who overcomes shall inherit all things, and I will be his God and he shall be My son" (Revelation 21:7).

Jesus told His disciples that "every creature" must be given the chance to hear and respond to the gospel, and whoever believes will be saved. As a sign to all, accompanying the preaching of the gospel would be the power to deliver people from demons, healing of the sick, supernatural protection and the outpouring of the Holy Spirit, which includes the gift of tongues being given to believers (Mark 16:15-18).

Jesus Christ was not crucified and raised again to life so we could have a dead religion! The Lord did not call people to Himself so we could get bored and tired of empty religious rituals! God calls us and has a destiny for us all (Ephesians 2:10). He wants us to surrender our lives to God, fully, unequivocally and completely (Romans 12:1-2), so the Holy Spirit can live through us, to reach the world with the gospel of Jesus Christ! God wants to empower us and transform us into the image of His Son (Romans 8:29). Paul explained it like this: 'For the Kingdom of God is not in word but in power' (1

Corinthians 4:20). Do you have the power of God operating in your life? God does not have a special plan for important people only, but for all Christians. Do you want to live a life in the Holy Spirit? Do you want to be made a branch in the Lord's vine? Would you like to experience Divine appointments and power for God's glory?

The Church is not a social club and our commission is not to entertain, or to meet together with no vision or purpose – we are called to reach the world with the gospel. To do this, intercessors must go ahead in spiritual warfare, as Paul explained: 'To the intent that now the manifold wisdom of God might be made known by the Church to the principalities and powers in the heavenly places, according to the eternal purpose which He accomplished in Christ Jesus our Lord' (Ephesians 3:10-11).

All who are called into this life of intercession will be formed into the image of Jesus Christ, by the Person of the Holy Spirit living in them, and they will walk in the light as overcomers. "What is an overcomer?" you ask. An overcomer is a person who has made a full and unconditional surrender of his or her self to the Lord Jesus Christ, and has invited the Holy Spirit to live His life through him or her for the glorification of Jesus. They do not live for self, they live for Christ. Everything they are and own belongs to the Lord, and they can testify with Paul, in truth that: 'I have been crucified with Christ; it is no longer I who live, but Christ lives in me; and the life which I now live in the flesh I live by faith in the Son of God, who loved me and gave Himself for me' (Galatians 2:20). An overcomer is a person who can sing, "I surrender all," or any other worship song, chorus or hymn of full devotion, without their conscience telling them that they are singing lies and calling it worship. It is a mockery to sing of such a surrender, when one remains in full possession of all one is and am, the syndrome of *me, myself and I* is sin.

These overcomers will not be religious, by any stretch of the imagination, and they will appear to some, to be very different than other believers. This is because they will be and need to be. Many Christians have become one with the world and those who are one with God are a threat to them. This is why Paul warned: 'Do not be conformed to the pattern of this world' (Romans 12:2), and Christ came to 'deliver us from this present evil age' (Galatians 1:4). We cannot be one with a world, which is in rebellion against the will and standards of God. Jesus said, "The world hates you" (John 15:19), because your light shines upon their evil deeds. Jesus said, "For everyone practicing evil hates the light and does not come to the light, lest his deeds should be exposed" (John 3:20).

The overcomers I am referring to will not be regular church goers as you think, satisfied with empty ritual or the status quo. They will know there is more and will want more of God; perhaps this is you? Contrary to popular belief, we are not serving God when we meet without Him, just for the sake of meeting, to do what we do once again. Jesus said, "The wind blows where it wishes, and you hear the sound of it, but cannot tell where it comes from and where it goes. So is everyone who is born of the Spirit" (John 3:8). In other words, the ways of the Holy Spirit in people's lives will be an affront to religious people, who hope if they turn up for a Sunday meeting, and tick a few boxes on prayer, worship and Bible reading, that God is pleased.

The apostle Paul wrote: 'And He [Jesus] died for all, that those who live should live no longer for themselves, but for Him who died for them and rose again' (2 Corinthians 5:15). Is this your testimony, you live for God and not for yourself?

God spoke to Amos to warn the Lord's people that He hates religious rituals, devoid of true worship (Amos 5:21-23). God used Isaiah to tell the people, "To what purpose is the multitude of your sacrifices to Me? ...Bring no more futile sacrifices.... Your appointed feasts My soul hates. They are a trouble to Me, I am weary of bearing them" (Isaiah 1:11-14). In these passages the Lord tells us how troubled He is by empty religious rituals, devoid of true surrender. They trouble God, just as the empty religion of the Pharisees and Sadducees troubled Jesus. The Lord knew those two sects were very religious and respected in society, but all their religion was a sham (Matthew 23:14-36).

If you accept the call to be an overcomer, filled with the Holy Spirit and emptied bit by bit of self – you will receive greater revelation and many shocks. The flesh life will fight for its life and the only answer is crucifixion with Christ, death to self. In addition, your eyes will be opened and like Jeremiah or Ezekiel, you will see the true spiritual condition of God's people. Religion wants everything to be 'nice' and 'easy,' but a Holy Spirit led life, walking in the Spirit means participating in spiritual warfare, which the Church is called and commissioned to participate in (Ephesians 3:10-11, Ephesians 6:10-18). This is a spiritual war of good versus evil. God has said that in the last days He will pour out His Spirit on all people (Acts 2:17), and everyone who calls on the name of the Lord will be saved (Acts 2:21). The Devil knows he is defeated, but continues to release hordes of demonic forces to blind the eyes of the unbelievers and bring them under demonic bondage (Luke 10:17-20, 2 Corinthians 4:4).

Just as the Devil entered Judas Iscariot (Luke 22:3), the Devil entered Adolf Hitler prior to World War II (1939-1945), to try to stop Jesus' last command, to, "Go and make disciples of all nations" (Matthew 28:18-20, Mark 16:15). At the Bible College of Wales, Rees Howells, his son Samuel[1] and over one hundred others, all became channels that the Holy Spirit entered, to fight the Devil's schemes. For our struggle is not against flesh and blood, but against the rulers, against the authorities, against the powers of this dark world, and against spiritual forces of evil in heavenly realms (Ephesians 6:12). God's plan is that through the Church, the manifold wisdom of God should be made known to the rulers and authorities in the heavenly realms (Ephesians 3:10-11). Rees Howells and his team of intercessors, fully understood this and went to war daily, on their knees. Led by the Holy Spirit they fasted, prayed and interceded, to bind the strong man and pull down his strongholds, releasing angelic forces to do battle with the principalities and powers of darkness (Daniel 10). They were full of the Holy Spirit and were overcomers. We are still in a spiritual war (Revelation 12:17), and there are many battles to be fought.

The Holy Spirit not only shows us how to pray, but also exposes falsehood to bring repentance, forgiveness and grace – if it is accepted by those who are guilty.

God is love and in 1 Corinthians 13 Paul explains what love truly is. The entire chapter is filled with wisdom and is worthy of diligent study. 'Love suffers long and is kind; love does not envy; love does not parade itself, is not puffed up; does not behave rudely, does not seek its own, is not provoked, thinks no evil; does not rejoice in iniquity, but rejoices in the truth; bears all things, believes all things, hopes all things, endures all things. Love never fails' (1 Corinthians 13:4-8).

All the fruit of the Holy Spirit – love, joy, peace, patience, kindness, goodness and self-control, all spring forth from His love (Galatians 5:22-23). In the past, I relied on being strong and tough, warring in my own strength, but the Holy Spirit taught me in a deeper way, that true spiritual warfare cannot be fought in the flesh, but only in the Holy Spirit through love. This lesson would be very important in the future, especially as the Lord showed me how many tares the enemy has sown amongst His people, in places you would never expect, just as Jesus taught (Matthew 13:24-30). I soon learnt that when you come face to face with a tare, what's in them, evil spirits, will recognise the Holy Spirit in you and will hate you for being God's channel. These evil spirits will hate you with a passion and have been known to growl/grit their teeth, and may even threaten you! The response of the flesh is to deal with the problem in the natural realm and hate them in return, but if you retaliate in the flesh, you will be defeated before you have even started. 'For though we walk in the flesh, we do not war according to the flesh. For the weapons of our warfare are not carnal but mighty in God for pulling down strongholds' (2 Corinthians 10:3-4).

Tares cannot be delivered, set free, but are separated at the end of the age by angels (Matthew 13:24-30, 36-43, Matthew 15:13). Tares are the Devil's agents in disguise. They are people (even *confessing* Christians) whose association, cooperation and participation in sinful practices and sinful attitudes bring them into alignment with the Devil's plans. By their wilful rebellion against God and His will (as revealed in the Holy Bible), they have come into alignment with the Devil's plans and have given themselves (even unknowingly) over to powerful deceiving evil spirits. Without breaking that alignment, it is irreversible! It is lawlessness and 'Wickedness' (personified as evil) and they are under a 'strong delusion' (Zechariah 5:8, Matthew 24:14, 2 Thessalonians 2:3-12). Also, 'rebellion is as the sin of witchcraft and stubbornness is as iniquity and idolatry' (1 Samuel 15:23a).

Chapter Eleven

Led by the Holy Spirit

Jesus said, "However, when He, the Spirit of Truth, has come, He will guide you into all truth; for He will not speak on His own authority, but whatever He hears He will speak; and He will tell you things to come. He will glorify Me, for He will take of what is Mine and declare it to you" (John 16:13-14).

Some Christians believe the work of the Holy Spirit in God's house will never be confrontational, this was not the experience of John the Baptist, nor Jesus or the apostles. John the Baptist called people to repentance and once called them a brood of vipers! Jesus faced the religious people with their hypocrisy, and overturned the tables of the money changers in the temple and drove them out with a whip for desecrating the house of prayer for all nations! The apostles handed people over to Satan so that they could be taught a spiritual lesson (1 Corinthians 5:1-5, 1 Timothy 1:19-20); nullified church membership for those who did not walk worthy and disciplined Christians who openly sinned (2 Corinthians 2:4-7, 2 Corinthians 10:6, 2 Corinthians 13:2, 10). Elders who have publicly transgressed need to be rebuked in the presence of the Church (1 Timothy 5:20). Godly leaders can rebuke those under them (who are younger than themselves) when they have strayed from the commands of God (2 Timothy 4:2, Titus 1:10-13, Titus 2:15), whilst an older person should be exhorted as a father, and not rebuked (1 Timothy 5:1). Even the Lord said, "As many as I love, I rebuke and chasten. Therefore be zealous and repent" (Revelation 3:19). Jesus stated that the unrepentant brother who has wronged you and refuses to hear you, your friends, or the Church, should be treated as a heathen or a tax collector! (Matthew 18:15-17). There is always an order and a process in dealing with Christians who have sinned and love can be tough.

Most believers are non-confrontational and few Christian leaders want to deal with tares. Yet, the New Testament has many examples and exhortations of confronting and dealing with problematic people within the Church. Even those who called themselves believers who should be avoided, or shunned because of their public sinful lifestyles or actions. The two letters to the Corinthians and the letter to the Galatians covers many issues. The apostle Paul is very clear in his instructions, concerns, denunciations, rebukes, discipline and corrective teaching to these two erring churches.

On my travels, the Lord has sent me to give prophetic words of encouragement, as well as words of warning or rebuke to individuals, churches and to those in leadership. The Holy Spirit will not relinquish the Church of Christ to the power of tares or disobedient leaders without a battle, and God needs Spirit led people for this. Also, God can fight against rebellious people! (Isaiah 63:10, Jeremiah 21:5, Lamentations 2:1-5).

If you welcome the Holy Spirit to lead you and live through you, it will be a challenge to many. Over the years, some have called me a spiritual gipsy/gypsy because of the way the Spirit led me to speak His word in many churches, others said I was doing the Devil's work or was deceived, when I was led to call for repentance. Very few could see that the Holy Spirit had an itinerant ministry for me, because there were few who could speak His word, or were bold enough to speak it, when needed. The Lord sent me to help others and He taught me in every situation He sent me to. He used me to help others and he trained and refined me in the process. When some of these churches rejected the Holy Spirit, the Lord left them to their own work until some of them closed, whilst others struggled on in the flesh. For me, it was on-the-job training, as opposed to being sat down and bombarded with sermon after sermon, with no action.

I was told more than once by church members that I was not really committed "to our church" because I did not attend every single meeting. Perhaps they were right; I was not committed to "*their* church" because I am committed to the true Church of Jesus Christ. Little did these people know that as they were meeting and witnessing yet another re-run of a powerless meeting from the past, that God was working in and through me and others, at the very same time, elsewhere. Whilst religious traditions prevailed, the Holy Spirit was at work. You might ask, "Why did you not tell them what the Holy Spirit was doing elsewhere, whilst they were meeting?" My only reply is to confess that my life is not my own and the Holy Spirit in me, is not answerable to any religious man or woman, or a religious spirit. Jeremiah was pressed to conform to a broken religious system, but he was in touch with God and could not. I was not told to try to explain or justify my actions to them, because it is the Lord who vindicates. Whilst many were meeting for the sake of meeting, the Holy Spirit was reaching out throughout the world, and I felt sincere sympathy for those who did not realise that their endless meetings did not glorify God, because He was not welcome.

In the last days the true Church and the false church are separating even further apart. The true Church will be deeply concerned to meet the conditions of discipleship, set forth by Jesus Christ in the Gospels, and will welcome the Holy Spirit in their midst to do His work. The true Church will live with eternity in mind and will set its mind on the things of God (Colossians 3:2). Meanwhile, the false church will outwardly be religious, but will say in its heart, "Don't bother us with Jesus' teaching on the cost of discipleship; He didn't mean that teaching was for us anyway. We've been called to be blessed and we don't want anything to interfere with the comfortable lives we're seeking to live. And, we don't want any of that fanaticism which happened with the Wesley's, Evan Roberts or Rev. Duncan Campbell[1] in those revivals; that's all over now. God doesn't speak today. Come on everybody, let's sing hymn 252, I surrender all."

The Bible is full of hard teaching which kicks against our flesh: loving our enemies, taking up our cross, turning the other cheek, walking in the fruit of the Spirit etc. Just read the Sermon on the Mount (Matthew 5-7). The Bible also contains a number of denunciations, calls to repentance or hard messages for people to wake up, change, go in God's direction and do His will. See Isaiah 58, Joel 1:13-14, Joel 2:1, 12-17. Other messages are:
- John the Baptist's message (Matthew 3:1-10).
- Jesus' message (Matthew 3:17).
- Peter's sermon (Acts 2:14-40).
- Stephen's sermon (Acts 7:1-54).

- The apostle Paul upset a lot of people by his godly preaching! (Acts 13:42-52, Acts 17:1-14).

In addition, how many of us have applied the following biblical commissions or admonitions:

Towards those who oppress us. Jesus said, "I tell you not to resist an evil person. But whoever slaps you on your right cheek, turn the other to him also. If anyone wants to sue you and take away your tunic, let him have your cloak also. And whoever compels you to go one mile, go with him two. Give to him who asks you, and from him who wants to borrow from you do not turn away" (Matthew 5:39-42).

If you are having a party or people round for a meal. Jesus said, "When you give a feast, invite the poor, the maimed, the lame, the blind" (Luke 14:13).

For a Christian who has sinned against you. Jesus said, "Moreover if your brother sins against you, go and tell him his fault between you and him alone. If he hears you, you have gained your brother. But if he will not hear, take with you one or two more, that 'By the mouth of two or three witnesses every word may be established.' And if he refuses to hear them, tell it to the church. But if he refuses even to hear the church, let him be to you like a heathen and a tax collector" (Matthew 18:15-18).

For people who say they are Christians, yet their lifestyle declare something else. 'But now I have written to you not to keep company with anyone named a brother, who is sexually immoral, or covetous, or an idolater, or a reviler, or a drunkard, or an extortioner, not even to eat with such a person' (1 Corinthians 5:11).

In relationship, a prospective marriage partner, or in a business setting. 'Do not be unequally yoked together with unbelievers. For what fellowship has righteousness with lawlessness? And what communion has light with darkness?' (2 Corinthians 6:14).

For the divisive person. 'Reject a divisive man after the first and second admonition, knowing that such a person is warped and sinning, being self-condemned' (Titus 3:10).

For the person who *refuses* to work, the lazy and idle. 'For even when we were with you, we commanded you this, if anyone will not work, neither shall he eat' (2 Thessalonians 3:10). C.f. Proverbs 22:13. Please note that verse 10 states: 'If anyone will not work,' not the unemployed who are looking for work, nor those who are ill, or those with a disability which may disallow them from employment. But those who refuse to work. The Bible is very clear about helping those who cannot help themselves (Leviticus 23:22, Leviticus 25:35-36, Proverbs 25:21, 1 John 3:17), and is equally clear about those who refuse to help themselves.

Workers should not despise their superiors and should use wholesome words. 'If anyone teaches otherwise and does not consent to wholesome words, even the words of our Lord Jesus Christ, and to the doctrine which accords with godliness, he is proud, knowing nothing, but is obsessed with disputes and arguments over words, from which come envy, strife, reviling, evil suspicions, useless wranglings of men of corrupt minds and destitute of the truth, who suppose that godliness is a means of gain. From such withdraw yourself" (1 Timothy 6:3-5).

Christians who oppose the teaching of the apostle Paul. 'We command you, brethren, in the name of our Lord Jesus Christ, that you withdraw from every brother who walks disorderly and not according to the tradition which he received from us' (2 Thessalonians 3:6). And: 'If anyone does not obey our word in this epistle, note that person and do not keep company with him, that he may be ashamed. Yet do not count him as an enemy, but admonish him as a brother' (2 Thessalonians 3:14-15).

For those in church leadership relating to elders who have openly sinned. 'Do not receive an accusation against an elder except from two or three witnesses. Those who are sinning rebuke in the presence of all, that the rest also may fear' (1 Timothy 5:19-20).

The perilous last days. 'But know this, that in the last days perilous times will come, for men will be lovers of themselves, lovers of money, boasters, proud, blasphemers, disobedient to parents, unthankful, unholy, unloving, unforgiving, slanderers, without self-control, brutal, despisers of good, traitors, headstrong, haughty, lovers of pleasure rather than lovers of God, having a form of godliness but denying its power. And from such people turn away!' (2 Timothy 3:1-5).

The Holy Spirit is the Spirit of Truth and teaches all that Jesus taught (John 14:17, John 16:13-14). But there is one very big difference; the Holy Spirit will live out the teaching of the Bible in and through those He is invited to enter, in each and every situation He leads them into. The truth is this, the Church with all its best evangelistic efforts, including the forgotten Decade of Evangelism is still having little or no impact upon communities. Churches are shrinking and shutting, instead of thriving in the Holy Spirit. This is a sign of God's judgment for disobedience, for a Church that does not reflect its Master, or obey Him, is no longer a lampstand for all to see (Revelation 1:20, Revelation 2:1). Tares have played their role in enabling this to happen and leaders have left them unchallenged.

The Holy Spirit working in and through overcomers, in revival or awakenings, will achieve more in the lifetime of the Holy Spirit's outpouring, than we can achieve in all our lifetimes of effort and fleshly planning! "This is the word of the Lord to Zerubbabel: 'Not by might nor by power, but by My Spirit,' says the Lord of hosts" (Zechariah 4:6).

To be led by the Holy Spirit means we cannot struggle and strive to enter into the calling God has for us. We must obey Him in all things and that is the only call. With the changes that took place because of the Charismatic Renewal and the subsequent outpouring of the Holy Spirit, with the gifts of the Spirit being made manifest, there was for some a tendency to still operate in the flesh, to struggle and strive, by whatever means, to be seen. Some Christians wanted the power (the gifts), but without responsibility, accountability or constraint of the Holy Spirit. Like the Church at Corinth, they moved in the gifts of the Spirit, but serious issues were still present in the Church, because individual members had not taken up their cross daily and crucified the flesh. The last days overcomers will be the opposite in spirit to those who strive to be in the limelight. They will do their best not to bring attention to themselves, because they will point to Jesus Christ alone, for the glory of God. 'For I determined not to know anything among you except Jesus Christ and Him crucified' (1 Corinthians 2:2). The apostle Paul wrote: 'For we do not preach ourselves, but Christ Jesus the Lord...' (2 Corinthians 4:5a). 'He who glories, let him glory in the Lord. For not he who commends himself is approved, but whom the Lord commends' (2 Corinthians 10:17-18).

The Holy Spirit led the apostles to reach the world. They did not follow their own plans and devise wonderful ideas; they prayed, fasted and sought the Lord.

- Jesus said, "For the Holy Spirit will teach you at that time what you should say" (Luke 12:12).
- 'The Spirit said to Philip, "Go near and overtake this chariot" ' (Acts 8:29).
- 'Now when they came up out of the water, the Spirit of the Lord caught Philip away, so that the eunuch saw him no more; and he went on his way rejoicing' (Acts 8:39).
- "Then the Spirit told me to go with them, doubting nothing. Moreover these six brethren accompanied me and we entered the man's house" (Acts 11:12).
- 'Then one of them, named Agabus, stood up and showed by the Spirit that there was going to be a great famine throughout all the world, which also happened in the days of Claudius Caesar' (Acts 11:28).
- 'As they ministered to the Lord and fasted, the Holy Spirit said, "Now separate to Me Barnabas and Saul for the work to which I have called them" ' (Acts 13:2).
- 'So, being sent out by the Holy Spirit, they went down to Seleucia, and from there they sailed to Cyprus' (Acts 13:4)
- 'For it seemed good to the Holy Spirit and to us, to lay upon you no greater burden than these necessary things' (Acts 15:28).
- 'They were forbidden by the Holy Spirit to preach the Word in Asia...they tried to go into Bithynia, but the Spirit did not permit them' (Acts 16:6-7).
- "The Holy Spirit testifies in every city, saying..." (Acts 20:23).
- 'They told Paul through the Spirit not to go up to Jerusalem' (Acts 21:4).
- 'When Agabus had come to us, he took Paul's belt, bound his own hands and feet, and said, "Thus says the Holy Spirit, 'So shall the Jews at Jerusalem bind the man who owns this belt and deliver him into the hands of the Gentiles' " ' (Acts 21:11-12).
- "The Holy Spirit spoke rightly through Isaiah the prophet to our fathers..." (Acts 28:25).[2]

Chapter Twelve

Tares and Presumption

Moses said, "Now why do you transgress the command of the Lord? For this will not succeed. Do not go up, lest you be defeated by your enemies, for the Lord is not among you... the Lord will not be with you." But they *presumed* to go up to the mountaintop.... The Amalekites and the Canaanites who dwelt in that mountain came down and attacked them, and drove them back as far as Hormah' (Numbers 14:41-45).

Like many others, I have been deeply troubled with the way a few in Christian media raise support. The outlandish claims of debt release, becoming wealthy, the salvation of your entire household, a healing, a miracle, a breakthrough, receiving the title deeds of your neighbour's house or car – *if* you send x amount of money, make a pledge or give NOW![1] These boasts and claims are in such contrast to the teaching and lifestyle of our Lord and Saviour Jesus Christ who had nowhere to lay His head (Matthew 8:20). The apostle Paul learnt how to be content in all circumstances, whether physically or mentally (Philippians 4:11-14). This included his times in prison, being beaten with rods, stoned, whipped, well fed or hungry, thirsty and when he was without clothes and cold, presumably in prison, and three times he was shipwrecked afloat in the sea! (2 Corinthians 11:24-28). Some of the outlandish claims can be heard on Christian TV during their appeals; perhaps they would be funny, if it were not for the fact that many of these fundraisers make unscriptural claims and prey on the fears of the young, naive, vulnerable or biblically illiterate Christians.

A non-Christian was given my telephone number by a brother in Christ. He was channel flicking and heard that he could be healed if he sent x amount to this Christian ministry on TV. The man was desperate, but thought it best to seek out a Christian before parting with his hard earned money and to ask his or her advice. He found a Christian who gave him my number. The man explained his predicament. I was able to share the gospel with this man (he needed salvation, before a healing, what would it profit if he gained the whole world but lost his soul? See Mark 8:36). I explained to the man that you cannot buy God's favour, blessing, anointing or a healing and that first and foremost, he needed to repent of his sins and to give himself unreservedly to Jesus Christ, and live for Him. The man was thankful for all I had said to him, but how many people, including non-Christians have been duped or switched over in disgust. The name of Christ is blasphemed (Romans 2:24), because of so called Christian workers who make appeals with unscriptural warrants, with false guarantees and empty promises. If these promises of debt release and financial breakthrough truly worked, then why are they asking you for money? Does it not work for them?

More than a decade ago, a Christian worker went to North Africa to share the gospel and to discreetly hand out Christian pamphlets and New Testaments. He was invited into the home of an English teacher and they had food together. The Muslim man said he had seen Christian TV before via the satellite, but stated, "They always want your money!"

In relation to Christian fundraisers and those in Christian media who raise support: Is it possible that a tare has somehow, slipped in unnoticed and lured others in to adopt their ways? Jesus warned this will happen (Matthew 13:24-30). A tare can be a lure, something which entices, a bate, with the power to attract others. They beckon you and draw you towards them – to ensnare you. They seduce you to their will – they are decoys of temptation. A decoy is something or someone, used to entrap others or distract their attention.

What happened throughout Israel's history was written down for our benefit. 'Now all these things happened to them as examples, and they were written for our admonition, upon whom the ends of the ages have come. Therefore let him who thinks he stands take heed lest he fall. No temptation has overtaken you except such as is common to man; but God is faithful, who will not allow you to be tempted beyond what you are able, but with the temptation will also make the way of escape, that you may be able to bear it' (1 Corinthians 10:11-

13). Presumption is to take God for granted; and a tare or a weed will do this, as it is a plant growing where it is undesired.

'Therefore, since we have this ministry, as we have received mercy, we do not lose heart. But we have renounced the hidden things of shame, not walking in craftiness nor handling the word of God deceitfully, but by manifestation of the truth commending ourselves to every man's conscience in the sight of God. But even if our gospel is veiled, it is veiled to those who are perishing' (2 Corinthians 4:1-3). If you wish to know more, please read, study and meditate on Jesus' teaching in Matthew 6.

Presumption is a sin that many in Christian leadership commit. After all this time, I can still hear what a missionary, who was out of touch with God, once said to me, "It's very simple, all God has to do is send the money and I'll get on with the work!" This is the sin of presumption.

After the twelve spies went into the land of Canaan, the Israelites rebelled and refused to fight for their inheritance. Then they changed their minds and said they would attack, but they were told not to go as it was too late. 'And Moses said, "Now why do you transgress the command of the Lord? For this will not succeed. Do not go up, lest you be defeated by your enemies, for the Lord is not among you. For the Amalekites and the Canaanites are there before you, and you shall fall by the sword; because you have turned away from the Lord, the Lord will not be with you." But they *presumed* to go up to the mountaintop. Nevertheless, neither the ark of the covenant of the Lord nor Moses departed from the camp. Then the Amalekites and the Canaanites who dwelt in that mountain came down and attacked them, and drove them back as far as Hormah' (Numbers 14:41-45). They went up without God's blessing or approval and were defeated in battle!

The sin of presumption means stepping ahead of the Lord, outside of His will, hoping to achieve the general directive, which the Lord has given, and it is sought by the power of the flesh, instead of by the leading of the Spirit. "But the person who does anything presumptuously, whether he is native-born or a stranger, that one brings reproach on the Lord, and he shall be cut off from among his people. Because he has despised the word of the Lord, and has broken His commandment, that person shall be completely cut off; his guilt shall be upon him" (Numbers 15:30-31).

For some, pride in the call is often the reason for their fall. The right attitude to have is this: 'Keep back Your servant also from presumptuous sins; let them not have dominion over me. Then I shall be blameless and I shall be innocent of great transgression' (Psalm 19:13). However, in the Bible we have a number of examples of presumption:

- 'And when He had removed him [King Saul], He raised up for them David as king, to whom also He gave testimony and said, "I have found David the son of Jesse, a man after My own heart, who will do all My will" ' (Acts 13:22).

- Psalm 51:1-11 is King David's confession of his sin of adultery: 'Create in me a clean heart, O God, and renew a steadfast spirit within me. Do not cast me away from Your presence, and do not take Your Holy Spirit from me' (Psalm 51:10-11).

- Samson and Delilah – she had just cut the seven locks of hair from his head, breaking his walk as a Nazarite (Number 6:1-21), and thus rendered Samson powerless against his enemies because the Spirit could not come upon him: 'And she said, "The Philistines are upon you, Samson!" So he awoke from his sleep, and said, "I will go out as before, at other times, and shake myself free!" But he did not know that the Lord had departed from him' (Judges 16:20).

- 1 Samuel 15:1-26 is the rebellion of King Saul, the Holy Spirit had departed from him and an evil spirit from the Lord came upon him! 'But the Spirit of the Lord departed from Saul, and a distressing spirit from the Lord troubled him. And Saul's servants said to him, "Surely, a distressing spirit from God is troubling you." ...And so it was, whenever the spirit from God was upon Saul, that David would take a harp and play it with his hand. Then Saul would become refreshed and well, and the distressing spirit would depart from him' (1 Samuel 16:14-15, 23).

- 'And it happened on the next day that the distressing spirit from God came upon Saul, and he prophesied inside the house. So David played music with his hand, as at other times; but there was a spear in Saul's hand. And Saul cast the spear, for he said, "I will pin David to the wall!" But David escaped his presence twice. Now Saul was afraid of David, because the Lord was with him, but had departed from Saul' (1 Samuel 18:10-12). Note that King Saul was prophesying under the influence of a distressing spirit!

We must accept God's work, His commands and commissions, which must be carried out exactly as He says, and in His timing. On the reverse side, when the Holy Spirit tells us not to go somewhere, or to cease socialising with someone (or a group), or not to attend a particular event – we must also heed His command. This is what it means to walk in the Spirit – we cannot be presumptuous and just do what we want, when we want, or we may become prey to the guidance of a tare!

'Do not be like the horse or like the mule which have no understanding, which must be harnessed with bit and bridle, else they will not come near you' (Psalm 32:9). 'If we live in the Spirit, let us also walk in the Spirit' (Galatians 5:25).

A man had been praying about a particular situation and the Holy Spirit told him to see me. We had known each other for decades and he explained his situation and asked for my prayers. The Holy Spirit gave me a word for him which I shared. He acknowledged it as a word from God and was the confirmation he needed. I also told this man that another person would try to talk him out of it, and thus lead him astray. Months passed before I met this man again. I asked him about the word and the implementation of it. He wanted to talk about other Christian things, but acknowledged that he had not done it, as another person had talked him out of it. I politely explained how he acknowledged it to be the word of God all those months ago, and now he had rejected it. It later transpired that the consequences for his disobedience was severe and sad to behold.

In spiritual warfare, you dare not, put your own interpretation on what the Holy Spirit says. If you are really serious about serving the Lord, in whatever way He chooses, you would be wise and well advised to read, study and meditate on 1 Kings 13, the man of God from Judah. Fast and pray, asking the Holy Spirit to show you what it's all about. Don't ask others, He wants to teach you, if you are willing to learn. Not everyone in the Body of Christ has a teachable spirit and it is not unusual to come across full-time Christian workers without the Holy Spirit, who seem to think they know all there is to know, based upon their studies of books on theology etc. Jesus would say to them, "Are you not in error, because you do not know the Scriptures, or the power of God?" (Mark 12:24).

It is a sad fact that people will frequently believe what they want to believe, that which they are comfortable with. Those who look for teachers to teach them what they want to hear or not to teach on that which they do not want to hear!

Some captains of the army asked the prophet Jeremiah for a word from the Lord, but when it came they rejected it. They stated that Jeremiah had spoken falsely (Jeremiah 42-43). Some hear what they want to hear and will follow their own deceptive heart (2 Timothy 4:3-4). Jesus preached on total commitment, however hard the cost, but many turned back and followed Him no more (John 6:44-66).

Some people are not sincere, whilst others are under the influence of the evil one. Whilst they might profess to be Christian, they are not.

- In Jeremiah's day, Judah ignored Israel's example of what happened to a backsliding nation. The Lord spoke through the prophet Jeremiah saying, "Judah has not turned to Me with *her whole heart, but in pretence*" (Jeremiah 3:10).
- 'Grace be with all those that love our Lord Jesus Christ in *sincerity*. Amen' (Ephesians 6:24). There is a counterfeit love of which the apostle Paul alludes to in this verse.
- 'For certain men *have crept in unnoticed*, who long ago were marked out for this condemnation.... These dreamers defile the flesh, reject authority.... *These are spots in your love feasts*, while they feast with you without fear, serving only themselves, they are clouds without rain, carried about by the winds; late autumn trees, twice dead, pulled up by the roots; raging waves of the sea, foaming up their shame; wandering stars for whom is reserved the blackness of darkness for ever' (Jude 4a, 8a, 12-13).[2]

Chapter Thirteen

Rebellious Leaders

'Then he brought me back to the door of the temple; and there was water, flowing from under the threshold of the temple toward the east.… He measured one thousand cubits, and he brought me through the waters; the water came up to my ankles. Again he measured one thousand and brought me through the waters; the water came up to my knees. Again he measured one thousand and brought me through; the water came up to my waist. Again he measured one thousand, and it was a river that I could not cross; for the water was too deep, water in which one must swim, a river that could not be crossed' (Ezekiel 47:1, 3-5).

Some Christians are called as evangelists to bring numerical growth to churches and the Kingdom of God. Pastors, as shepherds oversee the flock and keep them safe from wolves and false teachers or false prophets etc. Others are apostles who plant churches; teachers help build Christians up in the faith and grow in the grace of God, whilst prophetic voices are sent to instruct and to refine churches in God's truth and will.

Having led many people to the Lord in my early walk with God, as I grew in the grace of the Lord, He opened my eyes to the sin, rebellion and troubles within churches, in order to enable their repentance and restoration.[1] Some churches are bound by tares, others are hindered by the complacency of nominal born-again Christians, whilst some are bogged down by the disobedience of the leadership. One of the great sins of church leadership is their indifference to getting to know the Holy Spirit as a Person, to allow Him to possess all they are,[2] and their indifference or complacency to Jesus' Every Creature Commission (Matthew 28:19-20, Mark 16:15).

As both Jeremiah and Hosea found, the role of a prophet is not easy. We like to hear, "Peace, peace," but the Lord Jesus

Christ cannot be at peace with an indifferent and complacent Church. His exhortations, warnings and indignation at rebellion in His Church can be found in His letters to the seven churches of Asia Minor (Revelation 1-3).

In all my Christian life, I have been involved with lively churches, which moved in the gifts of the Holy Spirit, and was surprised when the Holy Spirit sent me on a four thousand mile round trip, with the express purpose of sending me to a very traditional church. This church, without the Holy Spirit was in terminal decline. It had lasted decades and was on the road to closure. To my surprise, the Lord showed me He had a plan to save and revive it. He showed me and others, what His plan was and how He would lead it back into health. The church took several steps in the right direction and it was beginning to grow.

After being there for a while, I was invited to be part of the small leadership circle. The Lord showed me I must fix the maintenance problems of the building, spending my time doing painting and other practical jobs. In addition, I began to teach the people how to welcome and receive the ministry of the Holy Spirit. One surprised visitor, knowing the traditions of the church said, "The Holy Spirit has come here too!"

After years of preparing the ground, fixing the building, teaching the people, prayer, repentance for the past and cleansing the building etc., we received prophecies and directions of God's plan for the church. We sensed we were on the path towards a revival, God would get the glory, Jesus would be exalted, the Holy Spirit would be given His rightful place, the congregation would be revived and many would get saved. The confirmation of this belief took place one evening, when in the leader's meeting, an unusual event took place.

As the leadership meeting was closing, where we discussed and planned the services ahead, the Holy Spirit came upon me and I was led into prolonged prayer, seeking God. I felt compelled to fall to my knees; the others were bent double, sat in their seats. There were only three leaders present in the meeting, but suddenly, as I knelt down in reverence, a fourth unseen Person entered the room. The atmosphere changed and none felt able to look up. The Holy Spirit, dare I explain, stepped in and it felt like He was walking amongst us. We were silent when He came in and the minutes became hours in His presence and we stayed till past midnight.

One of these leaders was a very traditional man, who had avoided all supernatural encounters with God, and chose this church because of its rituals and safe religion, and yet, even he was humbly touched by this encounter. As this fourth Person walked about the room, this traditional Christian was touched by Him and suddenly all the pain left his body.

As I had been praying for revival for over a decade and was called to help prepare this church for God's outpouring, I expected the pastor would be thrilled at this encounter, but he was greatly unhappy that his routine had been changed. To make sure this never happened again, he decided to re-schedule our leadership meetings to a time where it was impossible to linger in God's presence again. Why did he not want to welcome God in our midst?

A little time later, the Holy Spirit moved in His gifts during a prayer meeting, and the pastor made it very plain that he had no wish to take the church in that direction. Then, the church received a prophecy from an elder of another fellowship, who was related to our church secretary. The pastor refused to share it with the members of the church, despite it all being a positive word about the fellowship growing in numbers, through the work of the Holy Spirit. Then when the pastor was pressed by the Holy Spirit, who was seeking to move the church on, he finally confessed to a few leaders, that the only reason he became the pastor of this church was to top-up his final few years of income to gain his full pension!

One day the Holy Spirit spoke to me about this pastor and said, "Go to his house immediately," and when I arrived, he told me he had been praying for God to send someone. I found him with his head in his hands and he confessed, "I'm afraid that when I go home to heaven, I'll be meeting a stranger." For forty years, this man had preached and been the pastor of many churches, but he never truly cultivated his relationship with the Lord, and the Holy Spirit was a stranger to him. For decades people looked to him and all he had to give them, was what he had read from books. Was this man a tare, no, but he did not want to do God's good pleasing and perfect will – he was a rebellious pastor.

I have included this testimony and the following, not to discourage anyone, but to explain how only the Holy Spirit can reveal the true situation in any church. The most discouraging situation is to live in deception and be deluded, and this is why the Spirit of Truth must reveal the truth in any given situation (John 14:17).

In all the troubled churches the Lord sent me into, and they were of differing denominations, I noticed a two-fold manifestation of His will. First, He would use me to bring healing, deliverance, prophetic words and encouragement, 'Let my vindication come from Your presence; let Your eyes look on the things that are upright' (Psalm 17:2). By these and more, the Lord would show by works of power that I was His servant and could be trusted as such. Second, after the pastor or elders had seen God working in and through me to their benefit, the Holy Spirit would reveal His plan, which was not always easy, and then they had to make a choice to obey God or reject His revealed will. Additionally, every prophetic word, which gave direction would be accompanied by several confirmations, from unconnected sources.

The Lord sent me to another church to serve in the fellowship and the pastor said, "Your exactly what we've been praying for. We've been asking the Lord for a prophet and intercessor, and He's sent you." Over the next year, when this pastor and his wife faced any crisis, the Lord led them to me, and I was able to minister prophetic words, direction and helped them with deliverance. Once again, the Lord used me to help them and this prepared the ground for them to receive direction from the Holy Spirit.

On three occasions, this pastor came round my house. Each time I testified that the Holy Spirit had spoken to me, having told me that he was coming and what I was to share with him. On all these occasions, I asked him to spare the time to listen to what the Holy Spirit had given me for him; after all, it was the Holy Spirit who sent him! The Lord told me to remind him about his first calling, but he always told me that he was too busy to listen. Why did he treat the leading of the Holy Spirit with such informality and indifference? Eventually I said to him, "Why did you become a pastor, because your calling was to be an evangelist?" He later confessed this was true, but he chose not to have the time to receive the word God gave me.

As this man was unwilling to receive the word of the Lord, he continued as the pastor in his own flesh, and the church struggled from bad to worse. I saw the Lord trying to reach out to him, but he had stopped up his ears. In the end, he had a breakdown, as he worked nights to pay his bills and led the church in the week. Was this the work of a tare? No, this was rebellion and selfishness, the flesh uncrucified.

At another church in an affluent area, a young homeless man slept in the church porch at night to keep dry and out of the wind. Some of the congregation were concerned, but not for the right reasons, and raised the cry, "What can we do?" Large glass doors were made to order, at a considerable cost and hung in place, shutting off the porch from anybody who wished to shelter there.

At one church I attended for some time, I was invited along to see how the Alpha Course worked and to assist and share. For this church, it was a social event, a night out with a free meal from a highly qualified chef, rather than a friendly way to introduce people to Jesus Christ. One of the church members boasted that she had been on the Alpha Course five times! Another member gleefully stated that this church was the only evangelical one in the diocese, yet the Holy Spirit was not permitted to operate, was not wanted and the majority of those who attended were sadly not born-again, and had not passed from death to life, they were unregenerate.

An elder, responsible for evangelism had a great burden for the prostitutes that hung around outside the church he attended. The elder was so concerned that he spoke one evening to the congregation about this delicate situation, who was going to reach them with the good news? Later, the minister was approached, "I'll deal with it," he said, and spoke to one of the woman members about it. The following week all the prostitutes were gone, and the week after that, "Where are they?" the elder asked the minister, "Why have they not been invited into the warmth and given (a cup of) tea?" "Oh, I dealt with it, the ladies told them to move on!"

As I was tucked away in the hidden life of prayer, it did not hinder the work of the Holy Spirit from leading people to me. From time to time, strangers would be guided to my home and contact me by Divine appointment. One day, a pastor from Africa was walking down my road, a complete stranger and he came knocking on my door. He said, "Every time I have passed this house I felt the Holy Spirit prompting me to knock this door." He managed to find the confidence to knock and was pleased to find I was a believer, who was sold-out to God to serve Him full-time. The Holy Spirit gave me a prophecy for him and when I prayed with this brother, the Holy Spirit overpowered him, and all this took place within ten minutes of his arrival!

I was invited to speak to him and his friends a few days later at a church meeting and the Holy Spirit moved in great power. One woman testified that she had never known anything like it. She said since that day when the Spirit came upon her, "I've had my own personal revival for days!"

Once again, I saw the pattern of the Holy Spirit – first He would demonstrate His power and then the person He was trying to speak to, would acknowledge this power. This happened every time and then the Lord would give them a word (which they did not want to receive), but was necessary for true discipleship.

One day I was with this African pastor and I shared with him that God was giving him the opportunity to receive the Holy Spirit as a Person, to indwell him, possess him, lead him and guide him. This was the next step deeper in God's will, which the Lord wanted him to take. Like Ezekiel, the Holy Spirit is ever desiring to take us deeper into Him (Ezekiel 47:1-6), but in every step, there is a further identification with the cross, before we take a further step into Christ's resurrection. 'That I may know Him and the power of His resurrection, and the fellowship of His sufferings, being conformed to His death' (Philippians 3:10).

After I shared the *full cost* with this African pastor, which Rees Howells and others have paid to have this close walk with God, he went home and I heard nothing from him. Then one day he sent me an email explaining that he was too busy building his ministry, and he could not devote that amount of time to get to know God the Holy Spirit. Once again, this was rebellion against God. It was the manifestation of the selfish uncrucified flesh resisting the will of God, in order to promote 'my' ministry (3 John 9-11). Even Jesus, the Son of God was about His Father's business and did the will of His Father, not

His own! (Luke 2:49, John 5:30). Jesus said, "My doctrine is not Mine, but His who sent Me" (John 7:16).

In many of these situations, the Holy Spirit in me was so deeply grieved that I felt tormented by it myself. Peter wrote about people who lived in or taught error (2 Peter 2), and cited Sodom and Gomorrah as an example: 'And delivered righteous Lot, who was oppressed by the filthy conduct of the wicked (for that righteous man, dwelling among them, tormented his righteous soul from day to day by seeing and hearing their lawless deeds)' (2 Peter 2:7-8).

These hard lessons, which I learnt in different churches, took place over decades. I was pleased to learn how God reaches out to His people, but shocked how they often reject Him. Of the ancient people of Israel, the Lord said, "I have stretched out My hands all day long to a rebellious people, who walk in a way that is not good, according to their own thoughts" (Isaiah 65:2). 'Woe to those who go down to Egypt for help, and rely on horses, who trust in chariots because they are many, and in horsemen because they are very strong, but who do not look to the Holy One of Israel, nor seek the Lord!' (Isaiah 31:1). And, ' "Woe to the rebellious children," says the Lord, "Who take counsel, but not of Me and who devise plans, but not of My Spirit, that they may add sin to sin" ' (Isaiah 30:1). In my experience, this testimony is also true of churches, who are dismissive and complacent concerning the Every Creature Commission (Matthew 28:18-20, Mark 16:15), and think of church as a social club, instead of a house of prayer for all nations (Isaiah 56:7, Luke 19:46). Too many pastors and teachers ignore Jesus' teaching on the cost of discipleship and seem content to go on with religious routines, as if God did not notice. The body, if it can, has tried in many places to disconnect itself from the Head (Romans 12:3-8). Yet, I have found in almost every church, chapel or mission hall etc. that there are a few people, who have a good heart and are desperate to go further with the Lord, but don't know how.

The ultimate judgment of God is to turn people over to error because of their deliberate and wilful rejection of the truth!

- Beware of the "spirit of slumber" because of the hardening of one's heart toward the things of God (Isaiah 29:9-13 and Romans 11:8).

- King Saul had an evil spirit sent from God because of his continual disobedience (1 Samuel 16:14-15).
- Those who suppress the truth in unrighteousness, God has given up to the defilement of the flesh; they have been given over to a debased mind, and have exchanged the truth of God for a lie (Romans 1:18-32).
- God will send a strong delusion on those who do not receive the love of the truth, who have pleasure in unrighteousness (2 Thessalonians 2:7-12).[3]
- 'The Lord has mingled a perverse spirit in her midst; and they have caused Egypt to err in all her work, as a drunken man staggers in his vomit' (Isaiah 19:14).

Some of God's people can be so rebellious that God (or the Holy Spirit) will fight against them. God is full of mercy, compassion and longsuffering, but there can come a day, when enough is enough.

- 'In all their affliction He was afflicted, and the Angel of His Presence saved them; in His love and in His pity He redeemed them...but they rebelled and grieved His Holy Spirit; so He turned Himself against them as an enemy, and He fought against them' (Isaiah 63:9-10).
- 'Thus says the Lord God of Israel, "Behold, I will turn back the weapons of war that are in your hands, with which you fight against the king of Babylon and the Chaldeans...and I will assemble them in the midst of this city. I Myself will fight against you with an outstretched hand and with a strong arm, even in anger and fury and great wrath" ' (Jeremiah 21:4-5).
- 'Standing like an enemy, He has bent His bow; with His right hand, like an adversary, He has slain all who were pleasing to His eye; on the tent of the daughter of Zion, He has poured out His fury like fire. The Lord was like an enemy. He has swallowed up Israel...He has destroyed her strongholds, and has increased mourning and lamentation in the daughter of Judah (Lamentations 2:4-5).
- 'For the time has come for judgment to begin at the house of God; and if it begins with us first, what will be the end of those who do not obey the gospel of God?' (1 Peter 4:17).

Chapter Fourteen

Examples of Tares

'And I told them of the hand of my God which had been good upon me, and also of the king's words that he had spoken to me. So they said, "Let us rise up and build." Then they set their hands to this good work. But when Sanballat the Horonite, Tobiah the Ammonite official, and Geshem the Arab heard of it, they laughed at us and despised us, and said, "What is this thing that you are doing? Will you rebel against the king?" ' (Nehemiah 2:18-19).

In another church I was called to, I found out that the previous pastor had been lured into adultery by a tare and was expelled by the church. Whilst the new pastor was being sought, the numbers plummeted and one Sunday by chance, an out-of-work pastor *happened* to walk in, or so they thought. As innocent people, they did not realise that the pastor happened to walk in on several churches without a leader, and managed to find the elders each time and explained his line of work. They saw a Divine appointment, without considering that it could be a devilish one (see Nehemiah 13:4-9, Matthew 13:24-30). 'When Sanballat the Horonite and Tobiah the Ammonite official heard of it, they were deeply disturbed that a man had come to seek the well-being of the children of Israel' (Nehemiah 2:10).

This man was invited to become the pastor and two years past without any growth. At this point, I was led by the Holy Spirit to join this church because God had a work He wished to do there. After being there for a while, the pastor knowing my walk with God asked my advice if we should participate in a nationwide evangelistic campaign. He asked me to pray about it, and the Holy Spirit showed me how He would supply two full-time evangelists and two part-time evangelists to evangelise the whole area, at no cost to the church!

The pastor was living rent-free in the manse, with a good expenses package, and as he did not receive a wage, every penny (cent) counted. Nevertheless, he was happy for things to remain the same, without the evangelism taking place, as he was running his own business, as well as the church. This was the work of a tare, a wolf in sheep's clothing; refusing to see the local area evangelised because of the fear that the fellowship should grow from a new source. He had no reason to fear these evangelists because the work of an evangelist and a pastor are distinct, and complementary in the Church (Ephesians 4:11-15). These evangelists were going to give the shepherd (who was actually a hireling) a boost to the church, by new members and additions into the Kingdom of God.

In every church service there were prophecies and tongues given, but it was clear that by rejecting the revealed will of God, they had opened themselves up to the flesh, or worse, and now most of these manifestations were not inspired by the Holy Spirit. In a hope to display that all was well, the pastor would lead the meetings and manipulate others to prophesy or speak in tongues. Several times he urged one of his weaker elders by saying, "You've got a word, please give it now," and the elder looked confused and said, "No." The pastor replied, "Yes, you have." "No," insisted the elder. "Yes, you have!" the pastor insisted, and the elder crumbled and said, "Ok." Then tried to give a tongue or a prophecy out of his mind. It was very evident because he stumbled, struggled and was confused.

When these inconsistencies continued, the words that were spoken were *always* about everything being ok and that revival was soon to come, with no reference to the decision to reject the will of God to evangelise the area. One day, one of the men who had been there a very long time prophesied, "There's sin in this church, terrible sin," and I thought, 'That rings true and must be dealt with.' Nevertheless, the pastor refused to acknowledge the word or be reminded of it. The pastor had rejected God's plan to reach the area. After some years, the Holy Spirit told me to leave, because He had already left and the church closed a few years later (Revelation 1:20, Revelation 2:5), so no more people could be duped or deceived.

In another church, in a town far from where I live, I was invited to preach on two different Sunday services. I was warned that disunity had broken out, which led to a split. What I found is that often it is not what they tell you, but the *things they fail to tell you* which causes the problems. The elder who invited me to preach had been in his position for more than thirty years, but the congregation wanted a full-time pastor, not the enduring leadership of this elder, and those with him. Twice in recent years, he had interviewed two prospective preachers to be the pastor, and both times, he was the person who decided they were not suitable, but invited each one in their turn to be the church evangelist. Both candidates agreed, believing the Lord had opened the door, but both felt the overwhelming sense that this elder did not want them there, even after seeing conversions and a small but significant growing congregation, so they left. This routine of one man controlling took place for more than thirty years!

This elder recognised my calling and asked if I could pray and discern the will of the Lord, and like Jeremiah, when I gave it to him, he was not pleased (Jeremiah 42:20-21). The Holy Spirit told me that he should leave and let the others, whom God had sent, to get on with the work! Nevertheless, he insisted that he was the only person who could make this church viable, despite all the decades of failure.

Some months later, I received a phone call from this elder's wife, seeking to know exactly the word I was given by the Holy Spirit for him. When she heard it, she said, "That's not what he told me." Then she told me what had happened to him, after he had rejected the direction of the Lord. The elder was now close to a breakdown because the church had shrunk further to less than a handful and themselves. Yet the elder was still unwilling to let go, because, as I realised, he was a tare who for more than three decades had exercised full control over that church, as numbers dwindled.

Every word must be tested, and we must never step ahead of the revelation God has given us, even if a great man or woman of God gives us a direction, without it being tested and approved by the Holy Spirit. Of course, this will only work if you know the Holy Spirit personally and can hear His voice. We must also be careful of a 'Gibeonite deception,' this was where Joshua and the elders took what was said as being ok and correct, *without inquiring of the Lord* and the Gibeonites deceived them (Joshua 9:3-27). It is our responsibility to always check with the Holy Spirit to confirm or deny any leading we receive from another (1 Corinthians 14:29-33). Remember the man of God from Judah was misled by an old prophet and it cost him his life (1 Kings 13). If we spend our lives looking for others to direct us into God's will, instead of cultivating a strong relationship with the Holy Spirit, we may well end up starting out in the Holy Spirit, but ending up in the flesh.

The Bible tells us to 'test the spirits' (1 John 4:1), and warns us of: tares, wolves, accursed children, hirelings and false: prophets, teachers and apostles. Not all those who profess the name of Jesus Christ are genuine and loyal to the King and His cause. They have a variety of motives for teaching or preaching about Him and His message whilst cloaking their sermons or discussions in Christian verbiage, with phrases from Scripture interspersed. Satan has many followers infiltrating the Church, false apostles and false teachers (2 Corinthians 11:13-15). There are also those who will deny the power of God even in the day of visitation (2 Timothy 3:1-9). Whilst some so-called 'believers' are known as wolves, tares or accursed children (Matthew 7:15, Matthew 13:24-30, 2 Peter 2:14-15). Jesus warned of false prophets who will come in sheep's clothing but inwardly they are ravenous wolves. By their fruits we will know them (Matthew 7:15-20).

Jesus said, "Take heed that no one deceives you..." (Matthew 13:5). Those who say that they cannot be deceived, already are! Not all signs and miracles are from God. Jesus said, "For false christs and false prophets will arise and show great signs and wonders, so as to deceive, if possible, even the elect" (Matthew 24:4-5, 24), see also Mark 13:22-23. The apostle Paul wrote: 'I fear, less somehow, as the serpent deceived Eve by his craftiness, so your minds may be corrupted from the simplicity that is in Christ' by those who preach 'another Jesus,' 'a different spirit,' or 'a different gospel' (2 Corinthians 11:3-4).

Jesus said, "If you abide in My Word, you are My disciples indeed. And you shall know the truth, and the truth shall make you free" (John 8:31-32).

Chapter Fifteen

A Persecuted Christian?

'For I know this, that after my departure savage wolves will come in among you, not sparing the flock' (Acts 20:29).

Satan can and does plant his servants – tares into churches and ministries to cause division, confusion, strife and to siphon off money, time and resources away from God's work. A Bible College accepted a student from a Muslim country based on his written testimony and a reference provided by a missionary who helped disciple him. For two years the staff and students of the College prayed for this brother to arrive. They were told he had to go into hiding because of his conversion from Islam to Christianity. For many months he lived in a forest hiding from his persecutors – so they were led to believe.

The College authorities were overjoyed when the student was able to flee persecution and after two years he arrived safely at the College. However, the College was perplexed because the student turned up with his pregnant wife and children, which was contrary to the College rules. The College had limited accommodation for married couples and all those with children *had* to live outside of the College, but this man always had good reasons or excuses for all his troubling actions. The sponsor asked the College to help, and it rescinded its rule of 'no children' because of the exceptional circumstances.

Whilst this was all going on, over a two-three year period, a man from North Africa (an Islamic region) who had received an Arabic Bible renounced Islam and embraced Jesus Christ as his Lord and Saviour. With no Christian background or heritage he was offered a scholarship, to help him grow in the Christian faith and to protect him from persecution and potential martyrdom. This student arrived just before the start of term, whilst the man from the other Muslim country arrived later in the year. Despite the culture shock, the man from North Africa settled in well and observed how Christians live in community and attended his first church service. He began to make new friends and quickly grew in the fruit of the Spirit and the grace of the Lord Jesus Christ.

The other man from the Muslim country did not settle in. There was no appearance of walking in 'newness of life' (Romans 6:4), or 'in the newness of the Spirit' (Romans 7:6). His wife did not speak English and was not allowed to, and she wore a Muslim headscarf. The family had their meals in the communal dinning hall with the rest of the College community but ceased coming after some weeks. A specially made accommodation was hastily prepared for the family. The student would look-in most days to see how the work was progressing, yet not once did he offer to help the already overworked staff, but complained constantly and was ungrateful, not like a person who had lived in the forest for fear of his life. As one staff member later said, "Why was this one student the *very centre* of College life? He contributed nothing to the College except problems!"

Every student had to do practical duties, often as part of a team, yet this man refused to do his. Only after the dean of students intervened did he agree to do his duties, but he quickly reneged on his promise and was constantly troublesome.

The student did not want to mix with other men students, bar one, the former Muslim from North Africa, but *did* take an interest in the women students. They felt alarmed around him and agreed never to be left alone in his presence!

The student did not adhere to the Sunday service dress code and flouted many of the College rules. His wife and children did not attend the services when they were most welcome to, yet he was secretly visiting a local mosque! The student tried to claim various benefits, none of which he was entitled to on a student visa and was most angry when he was turned down.

His sponsor allocated him an allowance each month, which he quickly squandered. Unbeknown to other students, he asked, begged and borrowed from them, especially married students, all of whom who lived offsite and had children. He also solicited finances etc. from friends of the College, (those who attended the public meetings or who helped in various other ways, but who did not live onsite), and then began *demanding* help! His mail was diverted to the home of a friend of the College, even hand delivered mail arrived through the letter/mailbox, which aroused suspicion. Things came to a head when one of the friends of the College told him to stop abusing and taking advantage of those who were helping him.

The student caused disturbances during lectures on Islam and was very defensive of the Islamic religion, stating that what the Arab guest lecturer said was untrue. One of the College trustees warned him of his behaviour, it was unacceptable and certainly not Christian. He was aggressive when another lecturer in a passing reference mentioned the idol worship of the stone in Mecca. The other students were shocked by his defensive conduct.

The student became friends with the man from North Africa, and tried to lure him back into Islam, even taking him to the mosque. The student revealed his true intention and without shame or remorse, spoke about many things, including: his acts of adultery, his disdain for his wife, how to fleece and exploit Christians by pretending to be a needy and persecuted Christian, and other negative and ungodly things.

The man from North Africa told him that he had renounced Islam and embraced Jesus Christ as the Son of God, and was following Him and embracing what the Bible teaches, not the Koran (Quran). He would not go back to Islam and then the friendship broke down. The Principal later said that the spirit of Islam had got a hold of him; this was true, but in reality it had *always* had a hold on him! The entire profession of conversion, delaying his arrival into the UK until his wife was pregnant was all a front, a scam from the enemy to infiltrate a Christian Bible College, with a cunningly devised plan to obtain citizenship. A trustee of a Bible College who had a ministry to Muslims stated, "It is very common for Muslims to infiltrate Christian organisations." This was a tare directly from Satan who confessed to lying so as to deceive and fleece many people.

When the student was confronted over some of his actions, he alleged that a Muslim secret agent was pestering him and that he had to cooperate. This 'agent' also visited him at College; it turned out to be a man from the local mosque whom both the students had met! The student publicly denied any truths that were pointed out and persistently lied, denied or made excuses to stay at the College.

One night, the North African man was attacked after coming back from an Arabic-speaking church meeting via the student's flat. His 'friend' had asked to see him. Walking from one campus to the next, he was approached by a stranger who asked if he used to be a Muslim. "Yes," he replied. He was punched in the face and fell to the ground – the attacker fled. He was taken to hospital and had concussion. The police were notified of this religiously motivated attack.

After the attack, the student turned on the North African man and used to spit at him and call him infidel etc. He was very frightened of him, especially as he threatened to phone up his family in North Africa and tell them where he was and what he was doing. The men students were told to look after the North African man, to help protect him and not to let him walk alone outside of the College campuses.

The entire student body learnt a Christian worship song and at the end of term review, sung in front of a large audience. Only one person was unable to sing praises to God, the student looked very uncomfortable, some of the staff later commented on this.

A meeting was held between a senior College official, a staff member, the sponsor of the student and the North African man who had been verbally abused and attacked. The sponsor was stunned, shocked and horrified at all that had gone on and broke down in tears. The student and his family were going to fly back to their own country to sort out some things. At the airport (to protect the North African man), the sponsor told his student that he would not be coming back to the College and that the support would stop.

The student never came back to College, but convinced his sponsor that he had been the victim and that the other man was in fact the Muslim who tried to drag him back to Islam. Within a year, the student was back in the country at another Bible College. He had convinced his sponsor that he was the victim! After graduation, the North African man went to work at a Christian Mission, which was in the same city as the College in which the expelled student later attended.

Some time afterwards, at the Christian Mission, the North African man was introduced to a woman who was studying at the same Bible College as the student. He was still carrying on, much the same as at the first College!

Staff and students at the first College had prayed for more than two years that this 'persecuted Christian' from a Muslim country could come to the College and study. As one staff member said, "I believe that we prayed him in when it was not according to God's will, in the same way the Israelites demanded a king in the time of Samuel [1 Samuel 8:5-22] and it caused major problems with future consequences." All the misery, persecution and death under King Saul (see 1 Samuel chapters 8-31).

One Christian leader commented that it sounded like a "Gibeonite deception." Where Joshua and the elders took what was said as being true, *without inquiring of the Lord* and the Gibeonites deceived them (Joshua 9:3-27).

At around the same time, the pastor of the church where the Muslim student was now assisting, became concerned and contacted members of the first College, including senior staff. The pastor was horrified as he listened to the facts and stated, "I can't believe it, the people at the church will not like this." He was told that 'every testimony shall be established by two or three witnesses' (2 Corinthians 13:1), and it was suggested that he also contact former students and friends of the College to hear what they had experienced.

The pastor stated that the student had gone home to his own country but would be back in a few months. He contacted him and told him that based on the facts the church could no longer support him or permit him to help at the church, but he was welcome to attend the services because they had given references which allowed him to get his visa.

When the student returned to the church, the elders wanted to have a meeting with the Christian Mission worker from North Africa, his superior, and the student. The North African man was advised by several people not to attend the meeting. He had nothing to prove or defend; either the pastor believed what he had heard or he did not. If he did believe the testimony of the Christian workers (and those he contacted from the first College) then he had to deal with the situation as the spiritual leader in authority.

The church was divided and so were the elders; they did not want to believe that the student was a tare, a wolf in sheep's clothing, a Muslim in their midst. The pastor had fully investigated the facts but the elders did not really believe the pastor! The church reaped what they had sown – division, because they rejected godly counsel, by the testimony of more than three witnesses, all of whom were in full-time Christian ministry! They chose not to act on what they had. The meeting was held, but the student did not turn up, and he later made his excuses, as was his custom.

A few years later, the North African man was introduced to the daughter of the sponsor who revealed that her father had been deceived by the student and more unsavoury facts were revealed. I could not understand how so many Christians had ignored the alarm bells ringing in their spirits, nor used the gift of discernment to see beyond the deception. At first, I wondered how a committed Muslim could pretend to be a believer, even partake of communion, but an expert, a former extremist explained that the Muslim had followed the Islamic doctrine of taqiyya (al-taqiyya), which is "allowable deception," to conceal, lie or deceive to protect oneself and ultimately, to further Islam. All the money he duped from Christians hindered them from investing into God's work. When he left his accommodation, his deception was further uncovered by a great deal of material on Islamic prayer and teaching.

In the parable of the just and unjust steward, Jesus said, "For the sons of this world are more shrewd in their generation than the sons of light" (Luke 16:8). Because of our enthusiasm for the gospel, we can be so easily duped when we take people's word as gospel and ignore all the evidence which loudly declares contradictory truths. What does the Scriptures say? Jesus said, "You will know them by their fruit" (Matthew 7:16). When someone says they are a Christian, or a believer, or a disciple of Jesus Christ and so much is very wrong, then serious questions need to be asked.

Did anybody actually ask the student for his testimony and hear it firsthand? What happened, did he repent? Did he renounce Islam? What did he think of Jesus Christ and what did Jesus Christ mean to him? Was his Bible worn with use or in pristine unused condition? The man from North Africa went on to see many Arab speaking converts, he planted a church and is still walking strong with the Lord as a faithful witness for

Jesus Christ. He truly repented, renounced Islam and gave himself to Jesus Christ at much personal cost.

The ignorance or blindness to the student tare allowed a Muslim posing as a Christian to enter two Bible Colleges and several churches, where he ran amok and took large amounts of money away from Kingdom work for himself. This was a tare of exceptional ability who was able to deceive and dupe so many Christians, some of whom moved in the gifts of the Spirit, yet only a few could discern that something was drastically wrong. It was as if a veil had been drawn across people's eyes and they were unable or unwilling to see things in the light of Scripture and to accept the facts which were laid open for all to see.

Like the nation of Judah in the days of Jeremiah and Ezekiel, there were some hard situations and facts which the nation had to face, but they refused to acknowledge there was a problem and carried on as if everything was okay! Because of this, coupled with their perpetual sin and refusal to heed the prophets and the word of the Lord, they were on the receiving end of the chastising, chastening, disciplining hand of God. The nation was taken over by an invading pagan power, Jerusalem was ransacked, pillaged and destroyed, and those who did not die by the sword were exiled to Babylon (except the poorest of the poor who remained in the land).

Churches or ministries that operate without the Holy Spirit, (and some openly reject Him and do not permit their members to be baptised in the Holy Spirit, contrary to Scripture), are even more vulnerable, because to reject the Holy Spirit, the Spirit of God, is to make themselves willing victims to other spirits – demonic spirits.

Jesus said, "He who has ears to hear, let him hear!" (Luke 8:8b). Jesus said, "Behold, I send you out as sheep in the midst of wolves. Therefore be wise as serpents and harmless as doves" (Matthew 10:16). The apostle John wrote: 'Beloved, do not believe every spirit, but test the spirits, whether they are of God; because many false prophets have gone out into the world' (1 John 4:1).

- Jesus said, "Take heed that no one deceives you" (Matthew 24:4, Mark 13:5).
- Jesus said, "Take heed that you not be deceived. For many will come in My name, saying, 'I am He,' and,

'The time has drawn near.' Therefore do not go after them" (Luke 21:8).

- 'Let no one deceive you with empty words...' (Ephesians 5:6a).
- 'Now this I say lest anyone should deceive you with persuasive words' (Colossians 2:4).
- 'Let no one deceive you by any means; for that Day will not come unless the falling away comes first, and the man of sin is revealed, the son of perdition' (2 Thessalonians 2:3).
- 'These things I have written to you concerning those who try to deceive you' (1 John 2:26).
- 'Little children, let no one deceive you. He who practices righteousness is righteous, just as He is righteous' (1 John 3:7).

The Value and Importance of Truth

- Jesus said, "I am the Way, the Truth, and the Life. No one comes to the Father except through Me" (Jn. 14:6).
- God's Word is truth. Jesus said, "Sanctify them by Your truth. Your Word is truth" (John 17:17).
- John wrote: 'This is He who came by water and blood, Jesus Christ; not only by water, but by water and blood. And it is the Spirit who bears witness, because the Spirit is Truth' (1 John 5:6).
- 'Buy the truth, and do not sell it, Also wisdom and instruction and understanding' (Proverbs 23:23).
- Jesus said to the Jews who believed Him, "If you abide in My Word, you are My disciples indeed. And you shall know the truth, and the truth shall make you free" (John 8:31-32).
- Jesus said, "However, when He, the Spirit of Truth, has come, He will guide you into all truth; for He will not speak on His own authority, but whatever He hears He will speak; and He will tell you things to come" (John 16:13).
- Obey the truth. Peter wrote: 'Since you have purified your souls in obeying the truth through the Spirit in sincere love of the brethren' (1 Peter 1:22).
- Love the truth (2 Thessalonians 2:9-12, this Scripture is in a negative form).[1]

Chapter Sixteen

Revival or a Nativity Play

John the Baptist said, "I indeed baptize you with water unto repentance, but He who is coming after me is mightier than I, whose sandals I am not worthy to carry. He will baptize you with the Holy Spirit and fire" (Matthew 3:11).

The Holy Spirit spoke to me about going to the United States of America. He showed me very clearly that I was to go to a small town called Mount Horeb, in a particular state. It was named after the mountain in the Bible, which is first mentioned in Exodus 3:1. 'Now Moses was tending the flock of Jethro his father-in-law, the priest of Midian. And he led the flock to the back of the desert, and came to Horeb, the mountain of God.'

My family and I all went together. It turned out to be a real break. The Holy Spirit did of course use me and on the Sunday, we visited a very large church. The man on the door discovering that we were English, told a few people and we received a very warm welcome. Part way into the service the minister stopped preaching and said, "I believe the Lord wants the man from England to come to the front and speak." Before I had left for America, I purchased a pair of sandals in a sale and as the label stated they were in my size, I never tried them on in the shop. At home, when I did try them on, they did not fit me and the Holy Spirit told me they had to travel with me to the USA and He would show me who they were for.

As I began sharing from the front why we had come, the Holy Spirit said, "The sandals are for the pastor." Therefore, I asked my son to get them for me from our hire/rental car and proceeded to share with the pastor, and his flock, that the Holy Spirit wanted the pastor to wear them, as the sandals of the gospel of peace (Ephesians 6:15). The Holy Spirit was concerned that they had been through a difficult time as a church and things had not been handled as the Bible states.

To avoid it happening a second time, they must all walk in the gospel of peace, which surpasses all understanding, and loving one another as Christ loved them. 'But avoid foolish and ignorant disputes, knowing that they generate strife. And a servant of the Lord must not quarrel but be gentle to all, able to teach, patient, in humility correcting those who are in opposition, if God perhaps will grant them repentance, so that they may know the truth, and that they may come to their senses and escape the snare of the Devil, having been taken captive by him to do his will' (2 Timothy 2:23-26).

The pastor came forward and tried the sandals on, and they fitted him perfectly, which was a relief to me, because they acted as a confirmation to the word I had given him, and therefore the word was accepted as from the Lord. I also shared about the time we had lost a baby through a miscarriage and that the Word of God says, "God is not a man, that He should lie, nor a son of man, that He should repent. Has He said, and will He not do? Or has He spoken, and will He not make it good?" (Numbers 23:19). After I had finished speaking, a man ran up to me thanking me for all I had shared regarding our miscarriage. This man then placed a hundred dollar bill (£62) in my hand stating, "You will never know how much you have changed my life. Forgive me, I must get home as soon as possible and tell my wife."

My son had a chat with one of the church members who made a disparaging comment about the prophetic word I gave, saying, "I didn't have a clue what he was on about." This often happens when people come to church to be entertained; but if you turn up to meet God, having prayed for the speaker, in all probability you will receive something. Nevertheless, if you turn up in the flesh, as many do, you will be disappointed and confused when God speaks, as this man was.

While I was in England, preparing for my trip to the USA, the Holy Spirit told me that I would meet some Amish believers, and I did one morning, in the lobby of our motel. An Amish woman was selling some cushion covers etc., and I noticed the quality was very high. The woman asked, "Would you like to purchase anything?" and I replied politely, by saying, "No," but the Holy Spirit whispered, "Yes you would." Therefore, I turned to the woman and she asked, "Have you changed your mind?" "Yes," I said, and I purchased three cushion covers, at the cost of about $30 (£19). I handed over a hundred dollar bill. The woman had no change. The Holy Spirit whispered, "You don't need any change," so I told the woman, "Please keep it all." She smiled and exclaimed, "Praise the Lord! He promised me He would provide for me!" "What do you mean?" I inquired. "I have come here to see a chiropractor," she said, "but I did not have all the money I needed for the appointment, and the Lord told me to make an appointment and He would provide all I needed and He has."

As I reflect on this, I realise that a man in the church in which I shared gave me $100 (£62) and I gave the same amount to this Amish woman, who clearly had a strong relationship with the Lord and was sensitive to the Holy Spirit. As ever, I was a channel through whom the Lord could pass His money to others.

A few days later, the pastor of the church we visited, invited my family for breakfast and he was wearing the sandals the Holy Spirit had provided for him. They had received a clear word, and made attempts to follow it, but did they have a full heart, to pay the full price to have an outpouring of the Holy Spirit in their church or area? This pastor introduced me to a man whom the church employed to arrange the Christmas nativity celebration. I was surprised, because it was only July. They told me they wished it to be, "The biggest and the best ever," and it turned out this man was a professional organiser, who travelled once a week to them, all expenses paid. All this was very new to me, using the Lord's money to entertain the flock. Did this have anything to do with fulfilling Jesus' Every Creature Commission?

A few years later, it pleased the Holy Spirit to hide me away for a time in a small Baptist church, tucked away down a backstreet. It had only a handful of elderly people, mostly retired, and they were faithful with the same light that their fathers and grandfathers had received. They loved their traditions and loved to bake cakes and sell them to the people of the world at a financial loss, in an attempt to raise money for missionaries! They were good people, but people who had been taught tradition and many were not born-again. They had no real experience of the work of the Holy Spirit.

It was at this time, one Sunday evening that I was in the pulpit, very high up in this old traditional church building, where they liked the speaker to be, whilst the majority of the people still sat at the back, struggling to hear, then something happened. That night I noticed a couple who slipped in towards the end of the service. The Holy Spirit sent them to tell me that there was an outpouring of the Holy Spirit in Pensacola, Florida, USA, and I was instructed to go there as soon as I could arrange it.

I had been sent to Brownsville Assemblies of God, where there was a revival, an outpouring of the Spirit of God, which led to millions of people visiting the church, as God changed many lives. Some people queued from 4:30am, for a seat in the 7pm service![1] The meetings here were powerful because God was moving and therefore they became controversial. Satan never allows God to save so many souls and to change and touch people's lives, without calling forth his 'hidden' tares to fight. There are sleeping religious spirits in many who are planted in churches to oppose all those who are called to visit or welcome the Holy Spirit in such a way.

All who have read the history of Christian revivals and awakenings will know that Satan always opposes God's work and it is always controversial, as it was in the apostles' day, just like on the Day of Pentecost (Acts 2). So how can we know if some new move is from God or not? Is it a Divine visitation or a demonic delusion? If you want to know if something is from God, ask yourself: are people repenting, forsaking sin and turning to Jesus Christ, are they reading their Bible more, spending more time in prayer, living more Christ-like lives, embracing the cross and holiness, or are they having a knees-up, running wild and living for self?[2] Ask the Holy Spirit to show you. Don't follow the advice of religious people, who may or may not be in touch with God, because it may be the blind leading the blind (Matthew 15:14).

The internet is ablaze with people who are being used by Satan to oppose all the work of the Holy Spirit (who glorifies Jesus Christ), as the Devil vents his hatred and bitterness through them. As Jesus said, "You will know them by their fruit" (Matthew 7:16). In all these internet posts, including social media, your mobile/cell phone, books, or guidance being given by word of mouth, do you witness the fruit of the

Holy Spirit – which is love, joy, peace, patience, kindness, goodness, faithfulness, gentleness and self control (Galatians 5:22), or the fruit of Satan – division, jealousy, hatred, strife, restlessness, pride, bitterness, misery and accusation, etc.? (Galatians 5:19). The Devil's prime occupation is accusation – he is the accuser of the brethren! 'So the great dragon was cast out, that serpent of old, called the Devil and Satan, who deceives the whole world; he was cast to the earth, and his angels were cast out with him. Then I heard a loud voice saying in heaven, "Now salvation, and strength, and the Kingdom of our God, and the power of His Christ have come, for the accuser of our brethren, who accused them before our God day and night, has been cast down" ' (Revelation 12:10).

Far too many have walked outside of God's fold of obedience, that the only way they can feel better about their backsliding heart is to accuse others of being worse! 'An ungodly man digs up evil, and it is on his lips like a burning fire' (Proverbs 16:27). Some look *only* for the negative, amidst so much positive, and *only* talk, write or emphasise the negative as a means to denounce the whole. They reject and denounce the majority because of a minority (or a single event/incident).

Those in leadership must highlight error, mistakes and bad doctrine when it arises, to protect the flock, but the spirit in which we speak or write, can testify which spirit operates in us – the Holy Spirit, the flesh or demonic spirits. Is it to edify and correct in meekness and love or just to denounce and tear down? 'To whom have you uttered words? And whose spirit came from you?' (Job 26:4). On one occasion, the people of Samaria did not accept Jesus because He was on His way to Jerusalem. 'And when His disciples James and John saw this, they said, "Lord, do You want us to command fire to come down from heaven and consume them, just as Elijah did?" But He turned and rebuked them, and said, "You do not know what manner of spirit you are of. For the Son of Man did not come to destroy men's lives but to save them" ' (Luke 9:54-56).

God moved mightily in the Brownsville Revival (1995-2000) in Pensacola, Florida, as the gospel of Jesus Christ was preached. Around four million people came and heard Steve Hill's Christ-encompassing, cross-embracing messages of repentance and holiness, as tears rolled down his face. The Holy Spirit was outpoured and it became one of the longest continuing revivals in a single location in the last two centuries. It was not a series of evangelistic campaigns, but a true outpouring of the Holy Spirit, and when God comes amongst His people things will happen. Most people who left the church sanctuary went away desiring a closer walk with God and more of Him, others who were led into repentance and met the Saviour had their lives changed forever.

We received a very warm welcome from the staff of Brownsville church, and as I thought about what was happening at Brownsville, compared to what happened to the church I had visited when in America on a previous trip, I wondered, 'Why has the Holy Spirit chosen to visit here and not the other church? Was it because God found a man and others with him, willing to pay the full price for God's glory to come down, rather than to be entertained?' One got a revival, which changed lives and swept people into the Kingdom of God, the other got an expensive nativity play.

The pastor who had decided on a full-production nativity play was in no way a tare, far from it, however funds which could have gone towards the Great Commission, which Jesus spoke about before His ascension (Matthew 28:18-20, Mark 16:15), had evidently been diverted to a lesser cause. Millions of Christians because of the scarcity of Bibles are still without their own copy of the Word of God (especially in China), whilst more than two thousands languages do not even have a single portion of Scripture in their own language! Other Christians around the world, our brothers and sisters in Christ are persecuted for righteousness sake, for being Christian. Some are harassed, mocked, beaten, imprisoned, tortured, starved, sold into slavery or martyred for their faith. Millions of other hard-working Christians live a hand-to-mouth existence, especially in developing countries. Who is going to stand up for those who cannot stand up for themselves, be a voice for the voiceless, or help those who cannot help themselves? See Psalm 79:11, Proverbs 24:11-12 and Hebrews 13:3.

'Open your mouth for the speechless, in the cause of all who are appointed to die. Open your mouth, judge righteously, and plead the cause of the poor and needy' (Proverbs 31:8-9).

Chapter Seventeen

The Last Days

'The vessel that he made of clay was marred in the hand of the potter; so he made it again into another vessel, as it seemed good to the potter to make. Then the word of the Lord came to me, saying, "O house of Israel, can I not do with you as this potter?" says the Lord. "Look, as the clay is in the potter's hand, so are you in My hand, O house of Israel!" ' (Jeremiah 18:4-6).

One evening I was walking along a beach when I noticed a lump of jagged rock, which was once part of the cliff rock. It had broken away with a landslip and had been rolling around in the surf. There are times when the Holy Spirit speaks without words and this was one such time, and I knew I was to pick up the lump of jagged rock. The Lord said four times to Jeremiah, asking, "What do you see?" as He spoke to him through nature (Jeremiah 1:11). This white rock that I picked up was about the size of a man's hand, and as I proceeded along the shore, I found three more rocks, each one smaller, and smoother in looks and touch, than the one before. The last one had been transformed from the large rock substance that I first found, into a smooth pebble, measuring 4 cm in diameter. Time and tide, working with the elements had taken a large, jagged piece of rock, which once fell from the cliff and in the process of time, turned it into a smooth, useable pebble. This reminded me of how the Holy Spirit can take a rough person, that the Devil once controlled and shouted through (2 Timothy 2:26), and turn him or her into something that has been refined by God's fire, and becomes fit for purpose, that He can speak through.[1] The Lord is the Master Potter and we, like clay, must be remoulded into Christ's image (Jeremiah 18:2-7). The Lord will not force us to change, we must invite

Him to change us, and accept it when it is hard, as our natural selfish nature, is replaced for His Divine selfless nature.

Today, in this generation the Lord God is seeking to raise up and release men and women, like the first disciples, to walk in the power of the Holy Spirit, as Jesus did on earth. The Lord is seeking a return to New Testament Christianity and this is what truly inspired me when I first became a Christian. I was told that the same Holy Spirit who worked in Jesus and the apostles, is working in the world today, and we are to expect the same results (with tares thrown in along the way!). All these decades on, I can look back upon years of Divine appointments, set in the midst of my regular routines. These testimonies should not be exceptional, but should be part of what it means to be a disciple of Jesus Christ, see Mark 16:17-18, Acts 2:43, 1 Corinthians 4:20, 2 Corinthians 2:12 and 1 Thessalonians 1:5. Signs, wonders, miracles, gifts of the Spirit, are all part of normal Christianity; religion without power is what is abnormal and is a sign of spiritual decay, decline or even death.

Some of the people God is raising up, I believe, will experience the most unusual miracles like the apostles witnessed. Passports and visas will not hinder some of them, as they will be transported by the Holy Spirit, when necessary, as Philip was, from one place to another. 'Now when they came up out of the water, the Spirit of the Lord caught Philip away, so that the eunuch saw him no more; and he went on his way rejoicing. But Philip was found at Azotus. And passing through, he preached in all the cities till he came to Caesarea' (Acts 8:39-40). It was the same with Ezekiel: 'Then the Spirit lifted me up, and I heard behind me a great thunderous voice, "Blessed is the glory of the Lord from His place!" ' (Ezekiel 3:12).

Many true believers are praying for and looking forward to the promise of a global revival and awakening. Joel prophesied this outpouring about the last days when God pours out His Spirit (Joel 2:28-32), a final ingathering of the harvest before Jesus Christ comes again. However, let us not forget that Satan will not let God move in power without a fight. For some, it will be revival or riots, like the days of John Wesley, whilst others will be led to cast their shadows over the sick, like Peter and people will be healed to glorify Jesus

Christ (Acts 5:15-16). Our brethren in China, numerous countries across the Middle East and other parts of the world know what it means to be persecuted, and this is a sign of the end times, as well as, signs, wonders and miracles accompanying the preaching of God's Word, see 1 Corinthians 2:4-5.

If you think the end time outpouring of the Holy Spirit will be days of ease, as heaven comes to earth, then remember what happened in the apostles' days! The outpouring of the Holy Spirit led to great troubles, as well as joy (Acts 13:48-52). Tares will still be mixed in amongst the wheat! The Lord told us He did not come to bring peace, but a spiritual sword, separating the clean from the unclean, the saved from the rebellious (Matthew 10:34-39). Into this mix, the Devil will do all he can to bring confusion, by introducing counterfeit measures, as the Scriptures declare: 'The coming of the lawless one is according to the working of Satan, with all power, signs and lying wonders, and with all unrighteous deception among those who perish, because they did not receive the love of the truth, that they might be saved. And for this reason God will send them strong delusion, that they should believe the lie, that they all may be condemned who did not believe the truth but had pleasure in unrighteousness' (2 Thessalonians 2:9-12).

This great outpouring of the Holy Spirit, with deceptions taking place in other areas, will lead, as all revivals do, to another thrust of missionary endeavour to reach every creature with the gospel.[2] God desires all men to be saved (Ezekiel 33:11, Matthew 18:14, 1 Timothy 2:3-4), and has promised to pour out His Spirit on all flesh (2 Chronicles 7:14, Isaiah 44:3, Joel 2:28-29, Acts 2:16-21).

In some regions of the world there are unreached tribes of people living in jungles who are protected by law from outside contact. Especially in the Amazon jungles of Brazil and its bordering countries, where unreached tribes have been spotted from the air, or seen along the riverbanks. They have no immunity from "Western diseases" and contact with these untouched tribes, as history has proved, can wipe out large numbers from each tribe. To combat this, the Holy Spirit will call intercessors to pray for overcomers, who in turn will visit them, in the power of the Holy Spirit and speak to them in their own tongue, to share the good news of Jesus Christ with them, with signs following. The Holy Spirit's Presence in and over them will stop any germs or diseases attacking those with whom they share the gospel.[3] Sadly, a few in the enthusiasm of their own flesh, will go out and step ahead of their calling, by raising up their own support without the Lord, and will go on to dissipate the call by working on their own ideas. Some may well make contact with those unknown, but without the Holy Spirit's guidance and the miracles He supplies, they may well introduce them to the Devil's diseases (John 10:10).

Signs and wonders on there own will not be the evidence of the truthfulness of the last days servants of God, because, "If they do not speak according to this word, it is because there is no light in them" (Isaiah 8:20). The Bible will be your guide to test and discern, in the Holy Spirit who is from God or man, so you must get to know your Bible now! Read, study the Bible and meditate on passages of Scripture, see Psalm 119:15, 27, 48.

Those who have been called and sent forth by God will have the fruit of the Spirit bearing fruit in them. The Devil cannot counterfeit love because it is the fruit of the Holy Spirit, but he can and will produce counterfeit gifts in his vessels, sent to lead people away from Christ. Some of these people will be tares. This is why Jesus warned of false believers, "Beware of false prophets, who come to you in sheep's clothing, but inwardly they are ravenous wolves. You will know them by their fruits. Do men gather grapes from thornbushes or figs from thistles? Even so, every good tree bears good fruit, but a bad tree bears bad fruit. A good tree cannot bear bad fruit, nor can a bad tree bear good fruit. Every tree that does not bear good fruit is cut down and thrown into the fire. Therefore by their fruits you will know them. Not everyone who says to Me, 'Lord, Lord,' shall enter the Kingdom of heaven, but he who does the will of My Father in heaven. Many will say to Me in that day, 'Lord, Lord, have we not prophesied in Your name, cast out demons in Your name, and done many wonders in Your name?' And then I will declare to them, 'I never knew you; depart from Me, you who practice lawlessness!' " (Matthew 7:15-23).

If you accept the call to be a last days overcomer, the Holy Spirit will set a guard over your heart and tongue, and you will be expected to meet God's high standards of holiness. God said, "Be holy for I am holy" (Leviticus 11:44), and Jesus said, "Be perfect" (Matthew 5:48). Be warned, if you are called, chosen and commissioned to go, guard your tongue (Numbers 12:1-16, James 3:1-12). Once again, you will be well advised and wise to read, study and meditate on these Scriptures.

The Holy Spirit is very sensitive and He will leave you if you are not careful (Psalm 51:11). Most churches do not know who they are dealing with, when they casually speak of the Holy Spirit. I have seen on more than one occasion, film footage of Kathryn Kuhlman, a healing evangelist, whilst ministering on a platform, crying and pleading with the people not to grieve the Holy Spirit (Ephesians 4:30), because He was all she had. If He is grieved, He will leave.

Today, some in ministry have left the narrow road and chosen the broad road (Matthew 7:13-14). They have trusted in all of man's methods and this has grieved the Holy Spirit, and in so doing, they are struggling financially. They have agreed overdrafts, which is akin to paying a tithe to the Devil; taking money from believers and siphoning it from God's Kingdom, to give to the world. The overcomers which the Holy Spirit will enter will receive all they need (Philippians 4:19), as long as they are doing His work, His way, in His time frame, and they will live sacrificially like the apostles (1 Corinthians 4:9-13). Remember some of those recalled in the Holy Spirit's hall of faith, were the ones rejected and despised on earth, suffering great hardships for the Lord (Hebrews 11:35-40). 'Therefore let us go forth to Him, outside the camp, bearing His reproach. For here we have no continuing city, but we seek the one to come' (Hebrews 13:13-14).

Who is the Holy Spirit? Even though at times, there can be a special closeness to Him, as you abide with the Holy Spirit, you must never forget He is God. Paul warned: 'Do not grieve the Holy Spirit of God' (Ephesians 4:30). Anything you say, any vow or promise you make, He will remember. We have all known times when we have been so jubilant that we have spoken out without thought to what we said. He is so tender and loving, but also very strict about what we say or claim. We are human. He is not. He knows our motives and where they are rooted. The Holy Spirit has a sense of humour, but He dislikes all unreality. It is pointless to say to Him about some vow or promise, "I meant it at the time," because He knows that if we do not fulfil what we stated, we never did truly mean it. A vow is a binding contract (Psalm 56:12, Ecclesiastes 5:4-5, James 5:12). Whenever I have said to Him, "I love you Lord," He will smile so graciously and tenderly, because we only love Him in measure, but are not aware of it ourselves.

We are God's children and at times, act like young children who say to their father, "I do love you daddy," but what motives can hide behind such statements! Have they broken something? Do they want something? You cannot, dare not, treat the Holy Spirit like a human being, for He is not human. He is God's Holy Spirit, a Person, with His own will, which far exceeds yours. Peter said to Ananias, "Why has Satan filled your heart to lie to the Holy Spirit? ...You have not lied to man, but to God" (Acts 5:2, 4). He is strict, but He can also melt you in an instant, with His love, which is so pure and holy that it penetrates every part of your being.

It is my own personal belief that you can never truly come to know and fully understand the Third Person of the Trinity and His ways. If you have invited the Holy Spirit to introduce Himself to you, you will be *ever* learning and getting closer to Him, if you obey; but He ever remains God and we are only human. The Holy Spirit is continually doing all He can to reveal Jesus to us and bring Him glory, so the Spirit Himself will always be beyond us. Jesus said, "However, when He, the Spirit of Truth, has come, He will guide you into all truth; for He will not speak on His own authority, but whatever He hears He will speak; and He will tell you things to come. He will glorify Me, for He will take of what is Mine and declare it to you. All things that the Father has are Mine. Therefore I said that He will take of Mine and declare it to you" (John 16:13-15).

There have been occasions in my life when the Holy Spirit has drawn close to me and every time, I felt like Isaiah did. "Woe is me, for I am undone! Because I am a man of unclean lips and I dwell in the midst of a people of unclean lips; for my eyes have seen the King, the Lord of hosts" (Isaiah 6:5). I can tell you of one special time, when I felt Him touch my arm as we walked together late one night, in fellowship. How afraid and yet protected I felt by His presence. I dared not look up.

Who is the Holy Spirit? He is God on earth, here and now, the agent of revival, and in the light of Jesus Christ, we are transparent before Him. Fifty-one years ago, from the time I write, I walked with a small chain in my hand to hurt another, for all the wrong reasons; today, I walk with Him, as part of a great chain of grace, that reaches all over the earth.[4] This chain of God's grace and mercy, joined link by link by those surrendered and filled with Him, can be used to save others who are bound and chained here on earth.

As Isaiah prophesied of the Lord Jesus, "The Spirit of the Lord God is upon Me, because the Lord has anointed Me to preach good tidings to the poor; He has sent Me to heal the broken-hearted, to proclaim liberty to the captives and the opening of the prison to those who are bound; to proclaim the acceptable year of the Lord and the day of vengeance of our God. To comfort all who mourn, to console those who mourn in Zion, to give them beauty for ashes, the oil of joy for mourning, the garment of praise for the spirit of heaviness; that they may be called trees of righteousness, the planting of the Lord, that He may be glorified" (Isaiah 61:1-3).

What are we living for? To obey the Lord Jesus Christ, as the Holy Spirit reveals His will to us! What is the Lord's ultimate will? That the Every Creature Commission may be fulfilled! "As I live," says the Lord God, "I have no pleasure in the death of the wicked, but that the wicked turn from his way and live..." (Ezekiel 33:11). 'For this is good and acceptable in the sight of God our Saviour, who desires all men to be saved and to come to the knowledge of the truth' (1 Timothy 2:3-4).

Jesus said, "Go into all the world and preach the gospel to every creature. He who believes and is baptised will be saved; but he who does not believe will be condemned. And these signs will follow those who believe: In My name they will cast out demons; they will speak with new tongues; they will take up serpents; and if they drink anything deadly, it will by no means hurt them; they will lay hands on the sick, and they will recover" (Mark 16:15-18). Jesus said, "All authority has been given to Me in heaven and on earth. Go therefore and make disciples of all the nations, baptising them in the name of the Father and of the Son and of the Holy Spirit, teaching them to observe all things that I have commanded you; and lo, I am with you always, even to the end of the age" (Matthew 28:18-20).

Chapter Eighteen

The Challenge

'For David, after he had *served his own generation by the will of God*, fell asleep, was buried with his fathers...' (Acts 13:36).

God is looking for men and women after His own heart, who will do His will. 'As they ministered to the Lord and fasted, the Holy Spirit said, "Now separate to Me Barnabas and Saul *for the work to which I have called them*" ' (Acts 13:22). Being obedient to the Holy Spirit is not always popular, but it is very effective, and most rewarding, as the following people have testified in Scripture: Matthew, Mark, Luke, John and Paul, to name only five from the New Testament. In modern history, there are many the Lord Jesus used, like: Martin Luther, John Knox, John Bunyan, Jonathan Edwards, David Brainerd, John and Charles Wesley, George Whitefield, Howell Harris, Christmas Evans, William Wilberforce, Lord Shaftsbury, George Müller, William Chalmer Burns, Andrew Bonar, Charles Finney, Billy Bray, C. H. Spurgeon, Florence Nightingale, D. L. Moody, J. Hudson Taylor, William and Catherine Booth, Maria Woodwood Etta, C.T. Studd, Paget Wilkes, R. A. Torrey, Evan Roberts, Amy Semple McPherson, Rees Howells, George and Stephen Jeffreys, Marie Monsen, Samuel Rees Howells, Kathryn Kuhlman, Jean Darnell, Reinhard Bonnke, Luis Palau, John Kilpatrick, Steve Hill and _____. I have left a space for your name, if you are willing to be made willing? In addition, there is a warning of the personal cost: You will know sleepless nights; you will be assailed on occasions with doubt, fear, discouragement, intimidation and oppression. If it happened to Elijah and Jeremiah, it can happen to us (1 Kings 19:1-4, Jeremiah 9:2). If you are called and have decided to sign up to the school of the Holy Spirit, you may not be in the limelight of willing souls who have won many to the Lord, with signs and wonders confirming the preaching of the gospel; instead, like me and thousands of others, you may be hidden away for a season. One thing is for sure, if you become a true messenger of Jesus Christ you will be opposed and a tare or tares will try to scuttle your ministry and walk with the Lord.

Orville Gardener said, "When a prophet is accepted and deified, his message is lost. The prophet is only useful so long as he is stoned as a public nuisance for calling us to repentance, disturbing our comfortable routines, breaking our respectable idols, shattering our sacred conventions."[1] This is what happened to the apostle Paul who saw revival and riots, as well as John Wesley during the Evangelical Revival (1739-1791).[2]

G. D. Watson (1845-1924) was a Wesleyan Methodist minister and evangelist. He wrote: 'If God has called you to be really like Jesus He will draw you into a life of crucifixion and humility, and put upon you such demands of obedience, that you will not be able to follow other people or measure yourself by other Christians, and in many ways He will seem to let other people do things which He will not let you do.

'Other Christians and ministers who seem very religious and useful, may push themselves, pull wires, and work schemes to carry out their plans, but you cannot do it, and if you attempt it, you will meet with such failure and rebuke from the Lord as to make you sorely penitent.

'Others may boast of themselves, of their work, of their successes, of their writings, but the Holy Spirit will not allow you to do any such thing, and if you begin it, He will lead you into some deep mortification that will make you despise yourself and all your good works.

'Others may be allowed to succeed in making money, or may have a legacy left to them, but it is likely God will keep you poor, because He wants you to have something far better than gold, namely, a helpless dependence upon Him, that He may have the privilege of supplying your needs day by day out of an unseen treasury.

'The Lord may let others be honoured and put forward, and keep you hidden in obscurity, because He wants to produce some choice fragrant fruit for His coming glory, which can only be produced in the shade. He may let others be great, but keep you small. He may let others do a work for Him and get the credit for it, but He will make you work and toil on without knowing how much you are doing; and then to make your work still more precious He may let others get credit for the work you have done, and thus make your reward ten times greater when Jesus comes.

'The Holy Spirit will put a strict watch over you, with a jealous love, and will rebuke you for little words and feelings or for wasting your time, which other Christians never feel distressed over. So make up your mind that God is an infinite Sovereign, and has a right to do as He pleases with His own. He may not explain to you a thousand things which puzzle your reason in His dealings with you, but if you absolutely sell yourself to be His love slave, He will wrap you up in jealous love, and bestow upon you many blessings which come only to those who are in the inner circle.

'Settle it forever, then, that you are to deal directly with the Holy Spirit, and that He is to have the privilege of tying your tongue, or chaining your hand, or closing your eyes, in ways that He does not seem to use with others. Now, when you are so possessed with the living God that you are, in your secret heart, pleased and delighted over this peculiar, personal, private, jealous guardianship and management of the Holy Spirit over your life, you will have found the vestibule of heaven.'[3]

There is no glory for the flesh in this kind of life, but God is well pleased and you will learn to be His friend. Jesus said, "No longer do I call you servants, for a servant does not know what his master is doing; but I have called you friends" (John 15:15). Do you want to be a true friend of God? Do you want to fully surrender *all* and walk in the Spirit and be led of the Holy Spirit?

'I beseech you therefore, brethren, by the mercies of God, that you present your bodies a living sacrifice, holy, acceptable to God, which is your reasonable service. And do not be conformed to this world, but be transformed by the renewing of your mind, that you may prove what is that good and acceptable and perfect will of God' (Romans 12:1-2).

Thank you for reading this book, please write a short (or long) review on your favourite review site, and give a shout-out on social media – thank you.

Appendix A – No Revival!

The Devil, anticipating any move of God and those praying towards a heaven-sent revival, has already planted many of his tares in churches etc. who will rise up and oppose the work of the Holy Spirit. The following is from *Britain A Christian Country, A Nation Defined by Christianity and the Bible* by Paul Backholer.

I recall a church which held an all-night prayer meeting on Friday. It was very hard-going but many felt we had to press through and claim the promises God was offering to us, through prophetic words. For about eight months we met every Friday night till at least midnight, to seek God's face and cry out for revival. People in the church were inspired and the Sunday evening prayer meetings grew from a few to a great crowd. We all cried out to God and sought Him with such passion, as we responded to the prophetic guidance God gave us. Many of us were tired at playing church and re-running old meetings, without God's power present.

Some in the church were deeply troubled about the promise of a coming revival and one man was so fearful, that he spent a whole week with the elders, who finally encouraged him that it was a good thing to witness a Christian awakening! However, it was noticeable that this one person had drained much of the energy and vision from the leadership, and some did not turn up for the late night prayer meetings any more. In the Sunday meetings one said, "Now we've all got to calm down and pray one by one." Within a month the vision was dead and I marvel how one person, played a role in killing the prophecies and prayers of a whole church. Later he became a leader!

Jesus said, "The Kingdom of heaven is like a man who sowed good seed in his field; but while men slept, his enemy came and sowed tares among the wheat and went his way. But when the grain had sprouted and produced a crop, then the tares also appeared. So the servants of the owner came and said to him, 'Sir, did you not sow good seed in your field? How then does it have tares?' He said to them, 'An enemy has done this' " (Matthew 13:24-28).

I am reminded of another incident. One elder was burdened by the Holy Spirit to start meeting with other leaders, to repent for the sins of God's people, humble themselves and pray. It was noted that the conditions of 2 Chronicles 7:14 are: humbling ourselves, praying, seeking God's face and turning from wicked ways, which will result in the forgiveness of sins and the healing of the land. Nevertheless, it is observed that in many meetings Christians tend to quote 2 Chronicles 7:14, but rarely do we actually get around to meeting the conditions. Consequently, a few Christian leaders began to meet to fulfil these conditions. Soon word got out among Christian leaders in the area of what was happening, and one minister arrived saying, "I've heard you're meeting to pray for revival. I want to join, but I'm not coming to talk; we must pray or not meet at all."

At the first meeting this minister attended, he poured out his heart to God in Holy Spirit led prayer and repentance. For weeks there were times of very sincere repentance, intercession and seeking God in humility. As the weeks progressed more leaders from the area began joining and it was soon being hailed as a great achievement for Christian unity. More pastors, vicars and elder's began meeting, and as these new participants were senior in the area, they began to command a stronger influence.

Now the minister who had poured out his heart to God in his first meeting, returned with greater passion and cried out for God to move, and expressed his burden for the lukewarm, sinful and half-heartedness of the Church. Suddenly one of the senior minister's said, "Oh, no! You can't take that burden on you," and began to lecture the weeping minister on why there is no real problem, because of all that is being achieved.

The elders who founded the meetings, as led by the Holy Spirit, were now junior members and looked at each other in disbelief! Over the following months, humility, prayer, repentance and intercession all ceased, as the new leaders 'organised' the meetings. "Let's learn this new song," one said, another, "I've invited an outreach worker to tell us about his work."

In this example, the enemy used a few unmoved leaders to torpedo the times of intercession, which the Holy Spirit began with a few broken-hearted believers. Jesus said to them, "An enemy has done this" (Matthew 13:28). What lessons can we learn? Perhaps the lesson is that we must stop organising, networking and talking, and start weeping and repenting. If God joins people together, great, but beware the tare, who comes with a mission to kill, steal and destroy (John 10:10). John said, "They went out from us, but they were not of us; for if they had been of us, they would have continued with us" (1 John 2:19).[1]

Social Media
www.facebook.com/ByFaithMedia
www.instagram.com/ByFaithMedia
www.youtube.com/ByFaithMedia
www.twitter.com/ByFaithMedia

Sources and Notes

Chapter 1
1. From *Understanding Revival and Addressing the Issues it Provokes* by Mathew Backholer, ByFaith Media, 2009, 2017, page 126. www.ByFaithBooks.co.uk.
2. Excerpts from pages 123-124, 126 and 132 of *Understanding Revival and Addressing the Issues it Provokes* by Mathew Backholer, ByFaith Media, 2009, 2017.

Chapter 2
1. www.hgca.com/crop-management/weed-management/black-grass.aspx. Accessed 3 June 2015.
2. See *Holy Spirit Power – Knowing the Voice, Guidance and Person of the Holy Spirit* by Paul Backholer, ByFaith Media, 2013, 2017.

Chapter 4
1. See my autobiography: *The Holy Spirit in a Man: Spiritual Warfare, Intercession, Faith, Healings and Miracles in the Modern World* by R. B. Watchman, ByFaith Media, 2015, chapters 1-2.
2. For an account of the Welsh Revival (1904-1905) see *Revival Fires and Awakenings: Thirty-Six Visitations of the Holy Spirit* by Mathew Backholer, ByFaith Media, 2009, 2017, www.ByFaithBooks.co.uk, and the DVD *Great Christian Revivals* by ByFaith Media, 2008, 2016. www.ByFaithDVDs.co.uk. For more information about heaven-sent revivals, see *Revival Answers, True and False Revivals* by Mathew Backholer, ByFaith Media, 2013, 2017.

Chapter 5
1. From *Extreme Faith, On Fire Christianity* by Mathew Backholer, ByFaith Media, 2013, chapter 49.
2. For an overview of deliverance and ministry, see chapters 40-41 and 49 in *Extreme Faith, On Fire Christianity* by Mathew Backholer, ByFaith Media, 2013, 2017.

Chapter 6
1. From *Holy Spirit Power – Knowing the Voice, Guidance and Person of the Holy Spirit* by Paul Backholer, ByFaith Media, 2013, 2017, page 114.

Chapter 7
1. *Revival Fires and Awakenings: Thirty-Six Visitations of the Holy Spirit* by Mathew Backholer, ByFaith Media, 2009, 2017, page 160.
2. From *Holy Spirit Power – Knowing the Voice, Guidance and Person of the Holy Spirit* by Paul Backholer, ByFaith Media, 2013.

Chapter 10
1. See *Rees Howells Intercessor* by Norman Grubb, Lutterworth Press, 1952, and *Samuel Rees Howells: A Life of Intercession* by Richard Maton, ByFaith Media, 2012, 2017. For the history of the Bible College of Wales (1924-2011), see *Samuel, Son and Successor of Rees Howells* by Richard Maton, ByFaith Media, 2012, 2017. Samuel Rees Howells passed into glory in March 2004.

Chapter 11
1. For revivals under John and Charles Wesley, Evan Roberts and Rev. Duncan Campbell, see *Great Christian Revivals* DVD by ByFaith Media, 2008, 2016, www.ByFaithDVDs.co.uk.
2. From *Holy Spirit Power – Knowing the Voice, Guidance and Person of the Holy Spirit* by Paul Backholer, ByFaith Media, 2013, 2017, page 52.

Chapter 12

1. See *Prophecy Now, Prophetic Words and Divine Revelations for You the Church and the Nations: An End-Time Prophet's Journal* by Michael Backholer, 2013, 2017, chapters 14-15, Offensive Christian Workers and Unholy Gain and Financial Manipulation.
2. Some people are not sincere. The apostle John wrote: 'Little children, it is the last hour; and as you have heard the Antichrist is coming, even now many antichrists have come, by which we know it is the last hour. They went out from us, but they were not of us; for if they had been of us, they would have continued with us' but they went out that they might be made manifest, that none of them were of us' (1 John 2:18-19).

Chapter 13

1. See my autobiography: *The Holy Spirit in a Man: Spiritual Warfare, Intercession, Faith, Healings and Miracles in the Modern World* by R. B. Watchman, ByFaith Media, 2015, chapters 3-9.
2. See *Holy Spirit Power – Knowing the Voice, Guidance and Person of the Holy Spirit* by Paul Backholer, ByFaith Media, 2013, 2017.
3. *Discipleship For Everyday Living, Christian Growth: Following Jesus Christ and Making Disciples* by Mathew Backholer, ByFaith Media, 2011, 2017, page 46.

Chapter 15

1. Based on a list in *Discipleship For Everyday Living, Christian Growth: Following Jesus Christ and Making Disciples of All Nations* by Mathew Backholer, ByFaith Media, 2011, 2017, page 46.

Chapter 16

1. An account of the Brownsville Revival (1995-2000) can be found in *Revival Fire, 150 Years of Revivals* by Mathew Backholer, ByFaith Media, 2010, 2017.
2. For a fuller explanation of this, with a case example see chapter 23 of *Revival Answers, True and False Revivals* by Mathew Backholer, ByFaith Media, 2013, 2017.

Chapter 17

1. See my autobiography: *The Holy Spirit in a Man: Spiritual Warfare, Intercession, Faith, Healings and Miracles in the Modern World* by R. B. Watchman, ByFaith Media, 2015, chapters 2 and 4-6.
2. See *Global Revival, Worldwide Outpourings* by Mathew Backholer, ByFaith Media, 2010, 2017, notably chapters 5-7.
3. For a case example of protection from germs, and transportation in the Spirit see *God's Generals: Why They Succeeded and Why Some Failed* by Roberts Liardon, Albury Publishing, 1996, pages 182-185.
4. See my autobiography: *The Holy Spirit in a Man: Spiritual Warfare, Intercession, Faith, Healings and Miracles in the Modern World* by R. B. Watchman, ByFaith Media, 2015, chapter 2.

Chapter 18

1. *It's Time For Revival* by Gwen Shaw, Engeltal Press, 1988, page 56.
2. For an account of the Evangelical Revival (1739-1791), see *Revival Fires and Awakenings: Thirty-Six Visitations of the Holy Spirit* by Mathew Backholer, ByFaith Media, 2009 and *Great Christian Revivals* DVD by ByFaith Media, 2008, 2016.
3. Original book source unknown, though in the public domain.

Appendix A

1. *Britain A Christian Country, A Nation Defined by Christianity and the Bible* by Paul Backholer, ByFaith Media, 2015, pages 274-275.

www.ByFaith.co.uk

ByFaith Media Books

The following ByFaith Media books are available as paperback and eBooks, whilst some are also available as hardbacks.

Biography and Autobiography
The Holy Spirit in a Man: Spiritual Warfare, Intercession, Faith, Healings and Miracles by R. B. Watchman. One man's compelling journey of faith and intercession – a gripping true-life story. Raised in a dysfunctional family and called for a Divine purpose. Sent out by God, he left employment to claim the ground for Christ, witnessing signs and wonders, spiritual warfare and deliverance.

Samuel, Son and Successor of Rees Howells: Director of the Bible College of Wales – A Biography by Richard Maton. The author invites us on a lifelong journey with Samuel, to unveil his ministry at the College and the support he received from numerous staff, students and visitors, as the history of BCW unfolds alongside the Vision to reach Every Creature with the Gospel. With 113 black and white photos in the paperback and hardback editions!

Christian Teaching and Inspirational
Tares and Weeds in Your Church: Trouble & Deception in God's House, the End Time Overcomers by R. B. Watchman. Is there a battle taking place in your house, church or ministry, leading to division? Tares and weeds are counterfeit Christians used to sabotage Kingdom work; learn how to recognise them and neutralise them in the power of the Holy Spirit.

Holy Spirit Power: Knowing the Voice, Guidance and Person of the Holy Spirit by Paul Backholer. Power for Christian living; drawing from the powerful influences of many Christian leaders, including: Rees Howells, Evan Roberts, D. L. Moody and Duncan Campbell.

Jesus Today, Daily Devotional: 100 Days with Jesus Christ by Paul Backholer. Two minutes a day to encourage and inspire; 100 days of daily Christian Bible inspiration to draw you closer to God. *Jesus Today* is a concise daily devotional defined by the teaching of Jesus and how His life can change yours.

Samuel Rees Howells: A Life of Intercession by Richard Maton is an in-depth look at the intercessions of Samuel Rees Howells alongside the faith principles that he learnt from his father, Rees Howells, and under the guidance of the Holy Spirit. With 39 black and white photos in the paperback and hardback editions.

The Baptism of Fire, Personal Revival, Renewal and the Anointing for Supernatural Living by Paul Backholer. The author unveils the life and ministry of the Holy Spirit, shows how He can transform your life and what supernatural living in Christ means. Filled with biblical references, testimonies from heroes of the faith and the experiences of everyday Christians, you will learn that the baptism of fire is real and how you can receive it!

Revivals and Spiritual Awakenings

Revival Fires and Awakenings, Thirty-Six Visitations of the Holy Spirit: A Call to Holiness, Prayer and Intercession for the Nations by Mathew Backholer. With 36 fascinating accounts of revivals in nineteen countries from six continents, plus biblical teaching on revival, prayer and intercession. Also available as a hardback.

Global Revival, Worldwide Outpourings, Forty-Three Visitations of the Holy Spirit: The Great Commission by Mathew Backholer. With forty-three revivals from more than thirty countries on six continents, the author reveals the fascinating links between pioneering missionaries and the revivals that they saw, as they sought God for the "greater things" in a spirit of holiness & worked towards the Great Commission.

Revival Fire, 150 Years of Revivals, Spiritual Awakenings and Moves of the Holy Spirit by Mathew Backholer, documents in detail, twelve revivals from ten countries on five continents. Through the use of detailed research, eye-witness accounts and interviews, *Revival Fire* presents some of the most potent revivals that the world has seen in the past one hundred and fifty years.

Revival Answers, True and False Revivals, Genuine or Counterfeit Do not be Deceived by Mathew Backholer. What is genuine revival and how can we tell the true from the spurious? Drawing from Scripture with examples across Church history, this book will sharpen your senses and take you on a journey of discovery.

Reformation to Revival, 500 Years of God's Glory by Mathew Backholer. For the past five hundred years God has been pouring out His Spirit, to reform and to revive His Church. *Reformation to Revival* traces the Divine thread of God's power from Martin Luther of 1517, through to the Charismatic Movement and into the twenty-first century, featuring sixty great revivals from twenty nations.

Understanding Revival and Addressing the Issues it Provokes by Mathew Backholer. Many who have prayed for revival have rejected it when it came because they misunderstood the workings of the Holy Spirit and only wanted God to bless the Church on their terms.

Learn to intelligently cooperate with the Holy Spirit during times of revivals and Heaven-sent spiritual awakenings.

Supernatural and Spiritual
Glimpses of Glory, Revelations in the Realms of God Beyond the Veil in the Heavenly Abode: The New Jerusalem and the Eternal Kingdom of God by Paul Backholer. In this narrative receive biblical glimpses and revelations into life in paradise, which is filled with references to Scripture to confirm its veracity. A gripping read!

Prophecy Now, Prophetic Words and Divine Revelations for You, the Church and the Nations by Michael Backholer. An enlightening end-time prophetic journal of visions, words and prophecies.

Heaven, A Journey to Paradise and the Heavenly City by Paul Backholer. Join one person's exploration of paradise, guided by an angel and a glorified man, to witness the thrilling promise of eternity, and to provide answers to many questions about Heaven. Anchored in the Word of God, discover what Heaven will be like!

Christian Discipleship
Discipleship For Everyday Living, Christian Growth: Following Jesus Christ and Making Disciples of All Nations by Mathew Backholer. Engaging biblical teaching with fifty easy-to-read chapters spilt into six sections, to aid believers in maturity, to help make strong disciples with solid biblical foundations who reflect the image of Jesus Christ.

Extreme Faith, On Fire Christianity: Hearing from God and Moving in His Grace, Strength & Power – Living in Victory by Mathew Backholer. Discover the powerful biblical foundations for on fire faith in Christ! God has given us powerful weapons to defeat the enemy, to take back the spiritual land in our lives and to walk in His glory through the power of the Holy Spirit.

Historical and Adventure
Britain, A Christian Country, A Nation Defined by Christianity and the Bible & the Social Changes that Challenge this Biblical Heritage by Paul Backholer. For more than 1,000 years Britain was defined by Christianity, discover this continuing legacy, how faith defined its nationhood and the challenges from the 1960s onwards.

How Christianity Made the Modern World by Paul Backholer. Christianity is the greatest reforming force that the world has ever known, yet its legacy is seldom comprehended. See how Christianity helped create the path that led to Western liberty and laid the foundations of the modern world.

Celtic Christianity & the First Christian Kings in Britain: From St. Patrick and St. Columba, to King Ethelbert and King Alfred by Paul Backholer. Celtic Christians ignited a Celtic Golden Age of faith and light which spread into Europe. Discover this striking history and what we can learn from the heroes of Celtic Christianity.

Lost Treasures of the Bible: Exploration and Pictorial Travel Adventure of Biblical Archaeology by Paul Backholer. Join a photographic quest in search of the lost treasures of the Bible. Unveil ancient mysteries as you discover the evidence for Israel's exodus from Egypt, and travel into lost civilisations in search of the Ark of the Covenant. Explore lost worlds with over 160 colour pictures and photos in the paperback edition.

The Exodus Evidence In Pictures – The Bible's Exodus: The Hunt for Ancient Israel in Egypt, the Red Sea, the Exodus Route and Mount Sinai by Paul Backholer. Brothers, Paul and Mathew Backholer search for archaeological data to validate the biblical account of Joseph, Moses and the Hebrew Exodus from ancient Egypt. With more than 100 full colour photographs and graphics!

The Ark of the Covenant – Investigating the Ten Leading Claims by Paul Backholer. The mystery of the Bible's lost Ark of the Covenant has led to many myths, theories and claims. Join two explorers as they investigate the ten major theories concerning the location of antiquities greatest relic. 80+ colour photographs.

Short-Term Missions (Christian Travel with a Purpose)
Short-Term Missions, A Christian Guide to STMs by Mathew Backholer. *For Leaders, Pastors, Churches, Students, STM Teams and Mission Organizations – Survive and Thrive!* What you need to know about planning a STM, or joining a STM team, and considering the options as part of the Great Commission.

How to Plan, Prepare and Successfully Complete Your Short-Term Mission by Mathew Backholer. *For Churches, Independent STM Teams and Mission Organizations.* The books includes: mission statistics, quotes and more than 140 real-life STM testimonies.

Budget Travel – Holiday/Vacations
Budget Travel, a Guide to Travelling on a Shoestring, Explore the World, a Discount Overseas Adventure Trip: Gap Year, Backpacking, Volunteer-Vacation and Overlander by Mathew Backholer. A practical and concise guide to travelling the world and exploring new destinations with fascinating opportunities.

www.ByFaithBooks.co.uk

ByFaith Media DVDs

Revivals and Spiritual Awakenings
Great Christian Revivals on 1 DVD is an inspirational and uplifting account of some of the greatest revivals in Church history. Filmed on location across Britain and drawing upon archive information, the stories of the Welsh Revival (1904-1905), the Hebridean Revival (1949-1952) and the Evangelical Revival (1739-1791) are brought to life in this moving 72-minute documentary. Using computer animation, historic photos and depictions, the events of the past are weaved into the present, to bring these Heaven-sent revivals to life.

Historical and Adventure
Israel in Egypt – The Exodus Mystery on 1 DVD, 110 minutes. A four year quest searching for Joseph, Moses and the Hebrew slaves in Egypt. Join Paul and Mathew Backholer as they hunt through ancient relics and explore the mystery of the biblical exodus, hunt for the Red Sea and climb Mount Sinai. Discover the first reference to Israel outside of the Bible, uncover depictions of people with multicoloured coats, encounter the Egyptian records of slaves making bricks and find lost cities. The very best of *ByFaith – In Search of the Exodus*.

ByFaith – Quest for the Ark of the Covenant on 1 DVD. Join two adventurers on their quest for the Ark, beginning at Mount Sinai where it was made, to Pharaoh Tutankhamun's tomb, where Egyptian treasures evoke the majesty of the Ark. The quest proceeds onto the trail of Pharaoh Shishak, who raided Jerusalem. The mission continues up the River Nile to find a lost temple, with clues to a mysterious civilization. Crossing through the Sahara Desert, the investigators enter the underground rock churches of Ethiopia, find a forgotten civilization and examine the enigma of the final resting place of the Ark itself. 100+ minutes.

Christian Travel (Backpacking Style Short-Term Mission)
ByFaith – World Mission on 1 DVD is a Christian reality TV show that reveals the real experience of a backpacking style short-term mission in Asia, Europe and North Africa. Two brothers, Paul and Mathew Backholer shoot through fourteen nations, in an 85-minute real-life documentary. Filmed over three years, *ByFaith – World Mission* is the very best of ByFaith TV season one.

Notes